Why Bother Praying?

Richard Leonard, SJ

Keep praying!.

Richard Leonard

Paulist Press
New York / Mahwah, NJ

Cover design by Dawn M. Massa
Book design by Lynn Else

Library of Congress Cataloging-in-Publication Data

Leonard, Richard, 1963–
    Why bother praying? / Richard Leonard, SJ.
        p. cm
    Includes bibliographical references.
    ISBN 978-0-8091-4803-5 (alk. paper) — ISBN 978-1-58768-227-8
    1. Prayer—Christianity. I. Title.
    BV210.3.L46 2013
    248.3'2—dc23
                                                                    2012043757

Published by Paulist Press
997 Macarthur Boulevard
Mahwah, New Jersey 07430

www.paulistpress.com

Printed and bound in the
United States of America

Contents

CONTENTS

Contents

To my Jesuit brothers,
who by how they live show me why we pray.

Foreword

James Martin, SJ

What I like most about my friend Richard Leonard's wonderful books, and what I would suspect thousands of other readers like as well, is his unique ability to be clear and pastoral, blunt and faithful, provocative and consoling, all at once. His most recent book *Where the Hell Is God?* was a huge publishing success, not only because of its brevity, but also because it tackled head-on questions about suffering that are often spoken of in hushed terms, and with embarrassment or even guilt. It was a boon to those looking for straight answers to life's toughest questions.

Readers will be delighted to learn that his new book is written in that same clear style. Prayer is too often seen as a topic cloaked in mystery, and something that only the saints and mystics can do well. Indeed, whenever I speak about prayer to groups both large and small, I often conduct a fun experiment.

First, I'll ask people to close their eyes. Then I'll say, "Raise your hands if you pray."

Usually about three-quarters of the audience will raise their hands. (Needless to say, I'm speaking to religious audiences.) Then I'll say, "Keep your hands up if you think you pray *well*." Typically all the hands come down except for three or four.

Finally, I'll say, "Now keep your hands up if you think you pray *very well*."

All of the hands always go down.

Part of that response might be out of humility, but part of it, and this is corroborated when I ask the audience afterwards, is because people think that it's always the *other* person who is praying well. Even devout believers are tempted to think: "I'm sure I'm the only one that has difficulties with dryness and prayer, with not understanding exactly what is supposed to happen in prayer, with feeling that my prayer is inadequate. Surely other people close their eyes and are flooded with mystical graces."

In other words, most people think that only they don't pray well. Making matters worse, many books on prayer seem to be written as if the person reading it already understands everything about the topic. Quite a few are written in a style that makes it difficult for average believers to understand just what is being discussed.

Richard Leonard's new book is for everyone who wonders how to pray, everyone who wonders what happens when you pray, and everyone who wonders if God hears our prayers. Reading his book is like being able to ask an experienced priest, "Can you say that in a way that I can understand?" But Richard is a learned man, and not someone given to off-the-cuff or shallow comments about something as important as our faith.

As such, it's a wonderful contribution to the rich tradition of writings on Christian prayer, only this one is one that you'll be able to understand—and use.

James Martin, SJ, is a Jesuit priest and the author of several books, including The Jesuit Guide to (Almost) Everything, My Life with the Saints, *and* Becoming Who You Are (*Paulist Press*).

Introduction

I never thought I would ever write a book on prayer. The Lord knows that at this stage I am no mystic. In fact, given there are three ways of being canonized a saint—by heroic virtue, mysticism, or martyrdom—sadly the most assured way for me to make that list at the moment is the last one. I share with many other Christians the usual desolations, lack of discipline, and focus that make my own prayer life a very humble offering to God each day. That said, the original mountaintop religious encounters with Christ which marked my early life are still nurtured and nourished by my daily attempts to stay in communion with the Father, Son, and Holy Spirit. My prayer life is now more in the valleys than on the mountain tops, but that has been the case for most of the followers of Jesus most of the time, so I am in the very best of company.

So if my own prayer life gives me no bragging rights, then why write a book about prayer? At the risk of sounding like St. Luke and turning you, my reader, into Theophilus in Acts 1:1, this book emerges out of my earlier work, *Where the Hell Is God?* In that book, I explored how I have held on to faith in a loving God in the face of a terrible car accident that left my sister a quadriplegic. I said there that while I was writing in the area of theodicy—how we hold on to faith in a God of love in the face of pain and suffering—my book was not for academics. It came out of experience. My reflections clearly triggered something for many others because I have been quite overwhelmed by the number and depth of the letters I have received. They touched me very deeply. They challenged my thinking and I am the richer for the correspondence.

But not everyone was happy with what they read. To be fair, I said that I was writing squarely in areas of speculative theology and that greater minds than mine over the centuries have applied themselves to the same questions and have come to very different conclusions about them. The problem for me was that when I most needed their insights, I found some of their answers inadequate. I did not blame them for that. The vast majority of them did not have the benefit of contemporary biblical studies, theology, science, and psychology to lend a hand.

That said, there was one area that caused the greatest comment and the most objections. It was my chapter on prayer. More precisely, my interlocutors focused on my encouragement to "stop praying for rain." One very elderly farmer said that as much as he liked my book, "I have prayed about the rain one way or the other every day of my life. I can't stop now." For the record, I am delighted if others want to pray about the weather. I can't do so, because if God is a big meteorologist in the sky, then he seems very bad at it. We go from a drought to a flood in a matter of days.

This example of what I was trying to say about intercessory prayer became a neuralgic point for others to express their ideas about prayer. Many people outlined their reasons for why they are not troubled when their prayer is not answered, or when things get demonstrably worse. Some were familiar to me:

> "We were praying about the wrong things because God knows what we need rather than what we want."
> "There is a much greater plan God has for all of creation and we cannot hope to see the bigger picture."
> "It is only in retrospect that we can see what God was intending by what he did or failed to do."
> "Prayer is always answered, it's just that we can't see how."

"We may not like it, but sometimes God just says 'no' to
   whatever it is we are asking."
"God's answer to all prayers is Jesus Christ—end of
   story."
"God does not listen to selfish prayers."

Other people wrote to me with sincerely held views, but
I must admit I found them less than helpful; in fact, I personally reject them, not just because of what they say about prayer,
but because of what they end up saying about God's love and
goodness:

"Not enough people must have been praying for that
   intention."
"We have not prayed long enough or hard enough for
   God to hear us."
"We just don't have enough faith."
"God is testing us by not answering our prayer to see
   how much we love him."
"God says 'no' to keep us humble and so that we just rely
   on God's grace every day."
"God does not listen to sinners; you have to have a pure
   heart for your prayers to be heard."
"Unless you do penance as well as pray, then God will
   not answer your prayer because you are not serious."

In *Where the Hell Is God?* I came up with a short definition
of intercessory prayer: it is "prayer that asks an unchanging God
to change us to change the world." Some correspondents told me
that "this does not end up saying very much at all." This surprised me. In any and every important way, I do not change easily or quickly, so asking God to change me is not an insubstantial
matter; it is grace building on nature. This is especially true if I
want to stay changed. It invites God to enable me to get real

about the challenges in my life and the world, the obstacles in my living the life of grace, and face up to them with faith so that my prayer might have a concrete and evangelical end: to be on mission with Christ to change the world. In other words, to do what we ask every time we say the Lord's Prayer.

All this got me thinking more broadly about prayer, what it actually is in all its styles and forms, and how we might answer the often-heard question, "Why do you bother praying?" Although I will offer whatever tips have helped me along the way, this accessible volume is less about how to pray, and more about why we pray and what it does for us, for God, and for the world. I want to explore with you the context within which we pray, what is distinctive about Christian prayer and praying to Jesus, what communal prayers do, how Mary and the saints help us pray, and, finally, what the point of prayer is—sending us out with Christ to witness to the reign of God in our world.

I said at the start that my prayer life is not to be emulated, but because of that, I have great solidarity and empathy with any-one who struggles with it. Four gems of wisdom have helped me to keep persevering. My Jesuit novice master, Fr. Des Dwyer, SJ, is a very wise and compassionate man. Like me, and I think rather unusually for novice directors, he is an extrovert. He understood what I meant when I said that I was sure that most of the Church's traditions and prayer practices seemed to be "the revenge of intro-verts." I do not doubt for a moment the value there is in being able to do an hour's meditation with a straight back, regulating breath-ing, hands in one's lap, or, even worse, sitting on a prayer stool. It is just that these venerable styles of prayer are easier for introverts than for those of us who are more outgoing and look to stimula-tion from external things or objective considerations. Eight-day and thirty-day retreats, as much as I now relish them, once seemed to me to be delicious forms of torture devised by the spiritually introverted, who have had the upper hand in our tradition for a very long time. Sensing that it is can be easy to give up or cut corners when the way seems unnatural and too hard for little benefit, my novice master used to regularly say: "Each day some prayer, any prayer, is better than no prayer." As unrealistic as it is for most of us, the bad spirit convinces us that we should have a powerful and sustaining prayer life all the time. The perfect is the enemy of the good. Rather than give up on prayer, the good spirit encourages us to do what we can, from where we can, as we can. Some prayer is better than no prayer.

The second piece of wisdom that I have found sustaining comes from the most important book on prayer I have not read. That last sentence is not a typo. The reason I have never read the book is that I never got past its title and the preface. Fr. Frank Wallace was an Australian Jesuit who in 1991 published a book on prayer entitled *Encounter, Not Performance* (Newtown: EJ Dwyer). It changed my prayer life. Frank Wallace outlined that while he was always dutiful to Mass, meditation, the Liturgy of the Hours, the Rosary, and the Ignatian Examen, it was not until he had powerful experiences of his faith through the Cursillo and Marriage Encounter movements that he came to see that prayer was not about doing things to keep God happy; it was not about "performing," but about creating a space within which we can encounter the love of God. Frank would readily concede that while this encounter can happen in the spiritual duties he did so faithfully all his life, he also saw that these daily rituals do not necessarily lead to a deepening of the primary relationship to which they point.

Whatever we call prayer—praise, reverence, doxology, worship, communing, thanksgiving, confession, conversation with a friend, supplication, awe, intercession, wonder, listening, meditating, contemplating, or many other things besides—it is in every case an encounter with God.

Prayer is a means to an end, not an end in itself. The end

we seek in prayer is to encounter the presence of a loving God. Once we stop acting for God, putting on a show, and instead seek God's presence in prayer, then all sorts of possibilities open up. Prayer also provides the place wherein God can find us. God's creativity and desire for our good know no bounds.

The third piece of advice I live by is: if it helps, do it; if it doesn't, don't. It is a variation on the theme in St. Ignatius' Spiritual Exercises where he advises the retreatants to return to what gave them consolation again and again and to move away from what causes them desolation. In fact, this principle is not just about prayer, it is a way to live. Neither Ignatius nor I think some things are optional extras for Catholics: praying over the Bible and celebrating the sacraments, especially the Eucharist. Apart from these being the oldest ways of Christians praying, they bring God's presence to us in concrete terms, here and now. The way the scriptures are read or the sacraments are conducted can be less than wonderful, but the grace they bring is the same. My concern is that some people in their enthusiasm for a particular style, way, or school of prayer can insist that this is the only way for everyone. "If you want to be a good Catholic, then that's what you have to do." Well, you don't. It is an example of what Patrick O'Sullivan, SJ, calls the "hardening of the oughteries": we ought to do this, we must do that. Even if some venerable practices nurtured saints and martyrs, and we may be foolish to ignore their obvious benefits, there are, in fact, many ways to God.

The final piece of advice I live and pray by came in the Jesuit Tertianship, the third phase of Jesuit formation. These days you do it around your fortieth birthday. I was very blessed to have the great spiritual director and writer Fr. Bill Barry, SJ, as my tertian director. Bill is the author of classics on prayer and spirituality and many other titles, including *God and You: Prayer as a Personal Relationship*, and *A Friendship Like No Other: Experiencing God's Amazing Embrace*. Bill tells the story of the time while he was provincial superior of the New England Jesuits. Just before he was to leave for Rome for a very important international Jesuit meeting, he had trouble swallowing. The doctor found a growth on his vocal chords. He decided to have the radiation right away. The next summer, he made his retreat. He went in right after having had a very difficult meeting in his job as the local Jesuit boss. His cancer, as well as this meeting, weighed on him. His spiritual director suggested he pray upon Isaiah's first Servant Song, Isaiah 42:1–7. He spent the whole retreat on it and at one stage heard through this text: "You're wanted, not needed." One evening while he was outside walking, he realized, "I could be dead now." And in the mood of the retreat, he burst out laughing with the thought "and someone else would be provincial and the province would go on quite well without me."

Sometimes we are so frantic about being needed that we drive ourselves into an early grave. If we die the world will go on, maybe the lesser and worse for us not being there, but on it will go. The best prayer enables us to keep ourselves in check. Those we love and serve do not need us. Hopefully they want us, and they want us in the best shape possible for a very long time. A very good outcome of prayer is self-preservation. God does not need us either. God wants us.

Some people need much more structure, ritual, a focus, and more texts in their prayer than others do. Some people like knowing that how they are praying is in line with hundreds and sometimes over a thousand years of tradition. That's great. Others will never find that style of prayer helpful. As long as what we are doing is good in itself and is bearing spiritual fruit in our lives, then if it helps, do it; if it doesn't, don't.

Why bother praying? Because, while there are some very wise and venerable guidelines, there is only one absolute rule: Is what I am doing deepening my relationship of love with God, my neighbor and myself? That's what makes prayer so dangerous.

Chapter 1

The Pilgrim's Progress

The most important context within which I prayed, the time when I learned the most about prayer, was among the hardest physical situations I have ever been asked to accomplish.

When I was in Jesuit novitiate in the mid-1980s, the second-year novices were dropped a 125-mile (200 kms) walk from our first house in Australia at Sevenhill in the Clare Valley north of Adelaide, South Australia. The Austrian Jesuits founded it in 1850. It is, to this day, a parish, retreat house and, thank God, it's a very fine winery!

The second-years were given enough money for one emergency phone call, and a letter from the novice master for the police explaining who we were and what we were doing. We were, officially, vagrants. With a backpack and a sleeping bag, we had to walk the entire way begging for our food and accommodation each day. In the pursuit of board and lodging, we could not tell anyone who we were or what we were doing. We could not trade off being a Jesuit. The novice master told us that if someone invited us into their home, then, after they had established the extent of their hospitality, we could tell them who we were, so that they would not fear that they had welcomed Jack the Ripper to stay the night. If the homeowner, however, offered the garage and a sandwich and then found out we were Jesuits and then wanted to offer the guest suite and a meal at the dining room table, we were told we could not get an upgrade from economy to first class!

Those ten days were the only time in my life I've known hunger. During winter, would you let me into your house, let me sleep in your garage, or give me some food? I stayed in hostels for homeless men run by the St. Vincent de Paul Society, broke into abandoned schoolhouses, camped out in bandstands, and slept out under the stars.

On day six, I arrived in a small country town at seven p.m. in the teeming rain. I was soaked to the skin. I was drawn by the bright fluorescent cross that hung over what I was soon to discover was the Catholic church. There was nothing in the rules to say you could not beg from churches. I walked up the presbytery steps and introduced myself to the parish priest. After giving my spiel, I asked, "Father, I wonder if you might put me in touch with the local SVDP?" In his wonderful Irish brogue he replied, "You're looking at the local Vincent de Paul." So Father gave me $5 for dinner and $5 for breakfast, a towel for a shower, and a bed in the now-unused old schoolroom. Because he never let me into the house, I went on my way the next day without telling him who I was and what I was doing.

On the second last day of the pilgrimage, as it's called, I approached the biggest house in Auburn. There I met Mrs. Mary McMahon who proceeded to grill me about where I had come from, why I was in such need, and where I was going. I never told a lie, but being a good Jesuit I never told the whole truth either. After the interrogation she declared, "I think I can trust you," and ushered me into her home. She told me I could stay in the guest room, have dinner with the family tonight and breakfast in the morning, and then be on my way. I then told Mary who I was. To which she said, "Well, I'll be buggered! The Jesuits look after the church here from Sevenhill, and go to the Vigil Mass on Saturday nights." Then she changed. "You haven't been sent out as a Jesuit spy have you?" "No," I replied, "why would you think that?" To which she said, "Well, the Jesuits are always going on about a faith that does justice in the world, and I thought you lot must have been dropped all over the parish to see if we are practicing what they have been preaching." I assured her I was not a spy.

I complimented her on her extraordinary generosity, to which she replied, "Well, listen, sunshine—let's face it. I thought you were okay, because you are, without question, the most articulate, well-spoken beggar I've ever met in my life."

I had a great night with all Mary's family, and the next day I was on my way.

When I got to the village of Saddleworth in the late afternoon, I saw a woman weeding her front garden beds, so I went through her gate and gave out my spiel. "Hello, I'm Richard Leonard and I'm going through to the Clare district to get work on one of the wineries to get my passage back to Sydney. I have nowhere to stay tonight and nothing to eat and I am wondering if you could help me with either or both?" To which Mrs. Brisky looked up and said, "Are you the Jesuit who stayed with Mary McMahon last night?" "I am. That would be me!" I replied. "Yes, she gave me a call this morning and said to keep a good eye out for you on the road. That's why I'm weeding the front garden beds now. You are very welcome." That night the McMahon family came down and joined me and the Brisky family, and we had another wonderful dinner in the Riesling Valley of Australia.

When I arrived at Sevenhill the next day I wrote back to that generous Irish parish priest. "Father, you didn't know it but that night you looked after a Jesuit novice. If one day I am ordained a priest and I am half as good to others as you were to me that night, I will be very honored and proud indeed." When I got to the Jesuit novitiate there was a letter waiting for me from that priest. "The Jesuits taught me at school at Limerick in

Ireland. I hated every single minute of it. If I'd known who you were and what you were up to, I would have kicked your backside and told you to get yourself out of town. Even now the crafty Jesuits have got one over on me."

On that road, I learned more about prayer in those ten days than in the previous twenty-five years. It is not by accident that the life of prayer is often called a pilgrimage of faith; we are on a journey, with one another and God as companions. I discovered on the road to Sevenhill that living simply, penance and fasting (even if I had no option), being totally dependent on God's goodness through the undeserved kindness of strangers, and being on pilgrimage in the real world helped me feel close to God in a way I had never known before. I prayed for my daily bread, for somewhere to lay my head, and I was often overwhelmed with gratitude for the smallest kindnesses. While it was a stark context, that pilgrimage showed me that the clutter in my head, heart, and life often gets in the road of me finding God and allowing God to find me.

PRAYER IN THE HERE AND NOW

Before we talk about how we pray I think we need to talk about the multiple contexts within which we pray. At least in Western society, there are manifestly good people who show no interest in prayer, belief, or faith. Spirituality in all its forms is irrelevant to them. When I asserted this in a workshop recently, an elderly man at the back yelled out, "That's because they haven't suffered enough yet." As readers of *Where the Hell Is God?* will know, on many levels I am not happy with that response. While our level of self-satisfied comfort is a factor, maybe even an important one, we don't pray or have faith in God simply out of our pain, or to stop him from sending further suffering to us.

While prayer comforts us in our pain, I think our motivation for spirituality should be much more positive.

If we are going to bother praying, I think the contexts within which we pray are vital to understanding why some of us continue to find the life in the Spirit so enriching to our daily lives, and why others, sometimes those closest to us, are walking away.

In studies in Ignatian spirituality one of the major developments has been how Ignatius' idea of the composition of place, where I look to concrete things and actual people in the Gospel stories and see where I am led, has been matched by the idea of the composition of self. Given modern psychology, the process encourages us to briefly own at the start of any formal prayer the concrete situation and actual people who are shaping who we are and how we feel as we come to pray. Ignatius would have loved this. He was working on the text and dynamic of the *Spiritual Exercises* up to his death. He often thought others were better directors of his process than he was; principally Blessed Peter Faber, SJ.

Starting from where and who I am just makes sense. If I pray to encounter God's presence, then I'd better start with how I am. God already knows my situation, but it helps me also to become aware of what I bring to prayer, how I am feeling, and what obstacles might stand in the road of good communication today. Taking this excellent principle from the particular situation to the more general context—owning the wider background against which I pray and the obstacles therein—makes the process a little easier to understand.

PRAYER IS PERSONAL

The first context within which we pray is personal. Some of us make a fundamental error between private faith and personal faith. They are very different realities. The faith Jesus lived and invited us to share was about us assisting in the kingdom coming here on earth, as it is in heaven. While we must have vital, important private moments in our prayer, Christian faith is personal faith lived out in the public square.

If our personal prayer is an encounter, rather than going through the motions, then religious experience is what gives it its foundation, its heart. Without a religious experience I imagine prayer is throwing words on the other side of the wall hoping that someone's there, that the constant repetition of formulas and rituals, even when these are ancient and beautiful, might end up an act of the will and mind more than an affair of the heart and a movement of the emotions. An encounter, no matter how big or small, is the wellspring of personal faith in God. Rather than speak about this in the abstract, let me share my own experience.

I come from a very devout Irish Catholic Australian family. We are tribal. Where I grew up my life revolved around my large extended and smaller immediate family and the local Catholic church. I went to Catholic elementary, intermediate, and high school. I had an uncle who was a priest and many relatives who were nuns. Even though my schooling was throughout the rebellious 1970s, I never questioned God or the prerogatives of the Church. I was an altar boy, in the junior St. Vincent de Paul, the parish youth group, and the junior Serra Club. I was a proud Catholic. But I think my relationship was primarily to the tribe, to the Church, not to God. Until I was fifteen years of age, I was all about performance, not encounter. But that was soon to change.

I can still remember the day toward the end of 1978 when five young Catholics walked into my religious education class at St. Joseph's Christian Brothers High School: Peter, Judy, Maree, Vince, and Peter. They were all older than I was, eighteen to twenty-two. I knew some of them. They had been at school with my older brother and sister. As soon as they started speaking, I was captivated. They began by saying they had sat where we were sitting. They identified with us as being ordinary young Catholics searching for meaning and purpose. And then they told us how they went on a retreat that changed their lives.

One year before, a well-known and highly respected priest, Fr. Ray O'Leary, had returned to our diocese after serving in a country diocese in South Australia. Soon after arriving, he founded a prayer group at Holy Name parish. Convinced that young people should be offered a more personal relationship with Christ, he devised a retreat program taking Catholic students in their last years of high school, young workers, or those who were attending university away for the weekend. On the Friday night of the retreat, Fr. Ray would tell the young people that by the end of the weekend they should make a decision about their faith.

Word was out that some parents were shocked that their young people were given an ultimatum that included the possibility of rejecting their faith. Fr. Ray said that even though many young people went to Mass every week and were educated in the faith, he argued that Catholic youth have to make all sorts of decisions in regard to career, lifestyle, residence, studies, and relationships. Religion, he contended, often fell by the wayside, as either an issue not important enough to make a decision on, or one relegated to the personal shelf of neglect, possibly to be taken down and dusted off years later for a hatching, matching, or dispatching.

Fr. O'Leary said that this wasn't good enough. After years of Catholic education or CCD, the Church had to take the risk of calling for a personal decision for faith. Some of the young people consciously chose membership in the Church. Other students made the decision, which of course is never irrevocable, against believing in God, Christ, and the Church. The entire retreat process was based on the pivotal question in Mark's Gospel, "Who do you say that I am?"

The five young evangelists in my classroom had made at least one of these retreats. They were full of stories of how it changed their lives. Each of them reported having a deep encounter with God and an experience of their faith in Christ.

I had never heard any Australian Catholic, let alone a young adult, talk like this. Not only was their faith unashamedly public, they were palpably, infectiously happy. I knew these people. I could not dismiss them as Jesus-freaks or screwballs. They lived up the street from me, and indeed two of the four men had sat in the room where we were sitting only five years earlier. They were happy. I remember thinking that I had never seen any demonstrably happy Catholics talk about their faith like this. Our parish's associate pastor was a bit suspect in some quarters because he told genuinely funny and human stories in his sermons. I had seen serious, pious, loyal, concerned, and faithful Catholics, but not many who were manifestly joyous. I realized in that classroom that for people who are offered salvation in Jesus Christ, we can look awfully glum about it. I was hooked. They were sane and enthusiastic, and they relished the community they found with each other at Holy Name parish. It sounded like Acts 2 to me. Reflecting on the impact of their witness that day, I have always thought that if Catholics are really filled with the joy of Easter, then we should start by telling our faces about it!

I could not make the retreat they were promoting in four weeks' time, but I did make it in February 1979. We were challenged to think over and pray upon whether Christ was an idea, a historical figure, the inaccessible Son of God, a prophet, a good man who did good things, or was Christ the object of our passion, inviting us to follow his way, speak his truth, and live his life.

Fr. Ray was not the main presenter in the retreat conferences. He just gently presided over it. The young leaders gave almost all the talks because there is nothing as powerful as peer-to-peer ministry. These women and men kept reassuring the hundred neophytes that God is loving, forgiving, and merciful. It was as if I was hearing this for the first time. It gave me hope and confidence. There were extended periods of silence, wonderful prayer sessions that all culminated in a long and life-changing celebration of the Eucharist, after which we were asked if we chose Christ or not. We had a very discreet and Catholic version of an altar call where if we chose to step out in faith we came forward and then Fr. Ray and the young leaders used that ancient gesture of empowerment—the laying on of hands—and prayed over us. We were not sleep-deprived; there were no drugs, alcohol, or any other substances on that retreat. There was no pressure either way. We were told explicitly that we were free to say yes or no, but in saying yes, along with scores of others, I had a religious experience, a flooding of the heart.

Somewhere in having a religious experience, I went from being in the tribe, to understanding why the tribe existed at all. I had an encounter with the presence of God. The experience that weekend, and my subsequent participation in the Holy Name prayer group and parish saw me go from performance to encounter. I started to read the Bible, pray each day, and learn about different methods of prayer. The sacraments of Eucharist and penance went from rote rituals to deeply felt experiences of God's love. And I wanted to share it. Maybe too much. I am still trying to apply the virtue of prudence in my life.

Years later when I was reading Friedrich Schleiermacher, William James, and Rudolph Otto, they gave me a theoretical structure for what had happened that weekend. My personal mystical experience was an immediate consciousness of the Deity. Indeed Otto's famous dictum in regard to religious experience, the *mysterium tremendum et fascinas*, the mysterious encounter that is both frightening or overwhelming and fascinating at the same time, sums up what I encountered, and now, on my best days, what I can still glimpse.

I am happy to concede that the appeal to religious experience must itself be contextualized. In his article "When Experience Leads Us to Different Beliefs," Islamist Daniel Madigan, SJ, argues that if religious experiences can be seen as cross-cultural manifestations, study of these elements alone ignores that they are "mediated for us by a community and situated firmly within that community's tradition of belief." Madigan does not dismiss the reality of religious experience or its social and religious importance but argues it is "firstly an experience of oneself... assenting to or achieving insight into and finally giving oneself over to the vision of reality proffered by a community that lives by that vision...." Furthermore, he argues that mystical experience is "not so much a direct experience of God as an experience of believing." He concludes, "If religious experience appears to be a phenomenon common to all traditions, we cannot claim that it is because a single absolute or ultimate is clearly at work in them all. What gives these diverse experiences a tantalizing commonality amid all their differences is the fact that they are all instances of human persons being drawn into communal vision or hypothesis about reality." This neatly parallels my own experiences. My religious encounters, my prayer, are of God, my belief in God, and of the community who nurtures my faith.

PERSONAL IS SOCIAL

The other context in which we pray is social. And on that score in Western society religious experiences and prayer have never had less support. We need to acknowledge at the outset of this discussion that there are those who dispute the reality of what happened to me on that weekend and dismiss all religious experiences and any belief in God as manifestations or symptoms of a psychiatric disorder. One neuropsychiatrist argues that religious faith is partly aberrant perception and partly "belief pathology." In *Evolution and Cognition*, Ryan McKay says religious experiences can be put down to "individuals…[who] tend to be misled by untrustworthy sources of information, and/or tend to be prone to having their belief formation systems derailed and overridden by their motives (wish fulfillment being chief among them). Motives thus help to explain what maintains delusory beliefs once they have been generated by first factor sources."

There are, however, several other scholars, including some who have no religious affiliations and who began their investigations not believing in the truth of religious experience, prayer, and mystical claims, who have ended up, not uncritically, accepting that the phenomena were real. Joseph Maréchal in *Studies in the Psychology of the Mystics*, Louis Dupré in *The Other Dimension*, and Jacques Maritain in *The Degrees of Knowledge* fit into this category. The reality is that if prayer, religious experience, and mysticism are symptoms of a psychiatric pathology, then it is the most multilayered, multicultural, and cross-generational pathology ever. I concede it's possible.

ARGUMENTS AGAINST BELIEF

More recently Richard Dawkins and the late Christopher Hitchens have led a very vocal group denouncing every form of religious belief and all its attendant rituals and experiences as not only delusionary, but dangerous. There is no point running away from the impact they have had on Western believers and nonbelievers alike. These aggressive atheists would argue that prayer is a colossal waste of time because the entire religious edifice is nuts. We are just praying to imaginary friends.

One of the confounding ironies of some atheists' position is that they argue that religion has been violently intolerant of other people's nonbelief. With some notable exceptions, they have a strong historical case for this in Western society, and, sadly, in some parts of the world right now. However, over the last forty years, I would have thought that in Western pluralistic democracies tolerance for belief and unbelief has never been better. I have many atheist and agnostic friends, some of whom are the best living people I know. You do not have to be religious to be moral. My debates with them are almost always conducted with mutual respect. My problem with the more recent aggressive atheists is that when they rail against all forms of religion, they rarely make any distinctions or concessions. While they preach tolerance, it is for every other idea except a religious or faith-based one; they rightly assert the importance of their experience, while at the same time dismissing and denouncing anyone else's religious experience. I am not being uncharitable here (even to the dead). I have seen and heard some of these men in action and there is no dialogue, no inquiry, and no meeting point. Everyone who disagrees with them is deluded.

The way we conduct ourselves with our adversaries is a very good litmus test of who we are, by what values we live, and the effect of our prayer. As St. Thomas Aquinas so wisely taught, "…Every other virtue is charity essentially: but all other virtues depend on charity in some way." So it follows that if we want to effect change from a person whom we believe to be in error, charity and humility are very good places from which to mount our rebuttal. As Gandhi once said, "I love the New Testament and the Christian ideas about God and I would take the waters of Christian baptism tomorrow if I saw Christians practice what they preach."

The problem for aggressive atheists is that, as much I want to respect their position, in most Western democracies the majority of the electors claim to be Christian. No one forces them to say this, check the box on the census, or claim this allegiance. This may well change in the future, but given that the present majority of the population in most Western countries is Christian, it is not surprising that, to a lesser or greater degree, the majority is still comfortable to see Christian values enshrined in law, social policy, and practice.

I want to be fair here. Some moderate and generous atheists say that while they know there is more to life than what we can see and touch, they do not think religion adequately explains this in any helpful way. They find satisfaction and meaning in contributing to the cycle of life in the same way every other animal on the planet does: we are born, we live, and we die, embracing wholeheartedly the beauty of a finite life. They have no need to believe in life after death in order for life on Earth to have meaning, purpose, or direction. For these thinkers death remains a mystery, something to be contemplated and deeply respected, rather than a puzzle to be solved. If we are praying in the real world and cannot reply to some of these genuine challenges to faith, then it's no wonder the ranks of those without any belief are growing.

Richard Dawkins, however, goes further. He argues that because religion does not follow the rules of science it is insane (his word) to believe in any of it. He has been recently called the apostle of the ideology of scientism. The word *ideology* here is an important one. The more I read and hear the aggressive atheists, the more I am convinced that, while they may be railing against the idea of God, they are even angrier at the influence organized religion (Christianity in particular) has had on society. They may have many valid points to make in that regard. The impact of religion on society, like all major movements, is a mixed blessing. But it has not been, and is not now, all bad.

Dawkins argues that it is irrational to believe in anything else other than that which science can experiment upon, test, evaluate, prove, or disprove. I wonder how he deals with love, especially sacrificial love, where a religious or nonreligious person will give everything, even his or her life, for something or someone else. It can be totally irrational. It happens every day. The same applies to forgiveness, beauty, conscience, and most importantly, why we are here at all—if there is any meaning to our existence.

The aggressive atheists also argue that religion is the cause of all the things that have gone wrong in the world. All of them. As I said earlier, religion's critics have several good points in this regard. There is a litany of shame in the way Christianity has been lived and abused over two thousand years, and history is littered with its victims, because of an unholy alliance between distorted theology and political power. It would be good, however, if we had another two-thousand-year-old social institution like Christianity with which to compare and contrast how you fare after being around for so long. At the same time, it is equally tragic to note that strong atheistic aspirations lay behind the French revolutionaries, communists, Nazis, and even Pol Pot, whose histories are littered with a multitude of victims as well. At our worst, believer and nonbeliever have little of which to be proud.

Remembering that Christopher Hitchens said that religion poisons everything, it was at least churlish on his part not to acknowledge that organized religion has also been the cradle and promoter of extraordinary art, architecture, music, law, philosophy, and indeed science in its earliest days. Much more importantly, in nearly every Organisation for Economic Co-operation and Development country, the contemporary contribution of organized religion in regard to education, healthcare, and welfare is second only to government, with some of these good works undertaken with an army of generous faith-filled volunteers. More on this later.

I heard an aggressive atheist say recently that he could not and would not pray because he was an evidence-based human being. I must admit I wondered what the planet would be like if the approximate 5.7 billion religious believers in the world stopped praying. I think the world would be unlivable, not because our prayers are stopping God from doing terrible things, but because prayer changes us for the better, and so 5.7 billion human beings are potentially better for having prayed. I know being a believer is not the only way to be moral. I have said I know atheists whose moral lives are outstanding; I have also seen the evidence of people who pray. I know it sustains them in their faith, hope, and love. We need more of it, not less.

Finally, I take exception to the way Richard Dawkins finds a group of Christians somewhere in the world who believe in something outside the mainstream and then claims it as proof that this is what all Christians believe. It is a basic logical fallacy. For the record, of the estimated 2.2 billion Christians in the world 1.2 billion of these are Catholic. Despite what some of us were taught, we Catholics, at least since Vatican II, do not take the Bible literally.

Taking Richard Dawkins' favorite example of the creation of the world, we do not have to believe that Genesis is telling us anything we need to know about science. There are two stories there revealing a religious truth that God is the author of creation. I have no problem believing in a God who works in and through evolutionary biology. This tells me that God has worked slowly and patiently through all of history to bring the Universe(s) into being. It also tells me that God is not a divine magician, doing one amazing trick after another, but, rather, that God has set in motion elements that have, over all time and space, developed, grown, and built one upon the other.

So rather than the aggressive atheists finding groups of Christians who have a very different position to Catholicism on creation and the Bible, why not take as Christianity's position that of the majority denomination, especially when we also consider that a significant proportion of the world's six hundred seventy million Protestants and the vast majority of the world's two hundred thirty million Orthodox and eighty-five million Anglicans would share it.

ARGUMENTS FOR BELIEF

Though God cannot be proved nor disproved in the classical sense of a proof, there have been some venerable arguments proposed that helped some people in their prayer life. With all due respect to the libraries written on the following sentences, one of the oldest is from the eleventh century, wherein St. Anselm said if you can imagine the most perfect being then that being has to be God because God is greater than anything we can imagine. This is called the ontological proof for the existence of God.

The cosmological proof says that something has be the first cause of creation; that the world did not come out of nothing. That first cause is God, who was not created but exists.

The teleological proof holds that there is such balance in creation, in the multiple universes leading to the evolution of human life and self-consciousness, that there must be an intricate intelligence presiding over its order and development.

Others have put forward a moral argument where the moral sense within humanity reflects a greater divine law, of God.

Lastly, the experiential argument says that so many people have had religious experiences in all their varieties for so long, all over the world, that both the openness to God and the experiences themselves are a compelling case for the existence of God. Given my own experience, I find this a strong basis upon which I pray. But I know others who had similar experiences to the one I had on that retreat in 1979. In some cases, they had more dramatic and immediate outcomes, and yet today they would call themselves agnostics or atheists. It seems that religious experiences need an ongoing context within which to deepen them and give them application and newer meanings.

While not even claiming to be an amateur scientist, I personally find the argument from balance endlessly fascinating. While I have met many people who argue that all of our given creation is the outcome of random chance, I think that this position is also an act or leap of faith. In fact, I find this leap of faith into believing in randomness to be a greater act of faith than believing that a higher intelligence, which we call God, is the first cause of creation. I only have to think that if one single element on earth and in the Universe was not in place as it is, we would not exist as we do, we would not be here as we are. I cannot believe that the complexity and balance in creation, from the solar system to the unbelievable structure of a cell, results from chance.

Finally, while I enjoy looking to science to satisfactorily answer how we are here and from where we came, it cannot answer *why* we are here, why life matters, whether our life is worth anything at all, and where are we headed. Richard Dawkins says that the why question is a stupid one to ask, but humans have been asking it for thousands of years. I want it answered, and science can't do it. I do not want to be told that life is meaningless. Faith tells the opposite story.

An atheist once told me that believing in God is the same as when the majority of the world believed that the earth was flat. Science came along and changed it forever. It was not the best analogy for his case. Experience changed perception and shaped the science. Eventually everyday people went to the horizon and did not fall off, so the theory was embraced because everyone could potentially test it. These days, people who have had the benefit of a quality education, including some highly educated scientists, do not see a contradiction between faith and reason. They ask different questions and allow different experiences to shape the answers.

I started this chapter saying that the context within which we pray is very important. It has never been harder to have a prayer life, to talk about it to others, and to be public about it. Without a religious experience, our prayer is a series of spiritual exercises we do, hoping someone is there. After a Christian has a religious experience, we meet the object of our passion in an encounter of love. And once we know we are loved by God, it changes everything. Pedro Arrupe, the Superior General of the Jesuits from 1965–1983, expressed it this way:

> Nothing is more practical than finding God, that is, than falling in love in a quite absolute, final way. What you are in love with, what seizes your imagination, will affect everything. It will decide what will get you out of bed in the morning, what you do with your evenings, how you spend your weekends, what you read, whom you know, what breaks your heart, and what amazes you with joy and gratitude. Fall in love, stay in love, and it will decide everything.

Why bother praying? Because at its most basic, prayer is making space for God to love us, and, through the community of faith, inviting us to have the courage to return the compliment. It changes lives.

Chapter 2

To Whom Are We Praying?

The imagination has had a tricky history in Christianity. Just ask St. Ignatius Loyola and St. Joan of Arc. Each of them had major trouble with the Church officials of their day because of the central role imagination played in their prayer. In 1527 the Spanish Inquisition took an interest in the young Ignatius because they feared the model of prayer he used and taught was that of the *alumbrados*, a movement of the time that argued no one needed the Church or the sacraments to have a direct and immediate experience of God and the Trinity. They came to a terrible end. Ignatius did share with this movement a strong belief in the role that imagination played in placing oneself in the presence of God, in being with Jesus in the stories of the Gospels, and in speaking to God personally, intimately. He was let off with a caution. St. Joan of Arc was burned at the stake for her politics as much as for her theology, but she always spoke of the way God spoke to her. "When I was thirteen years old, I had a Voice from God to help me govern my conduct....My prayer to God finished, I hear a Voice that says to me: 'Daughter of God, go, go, go; I will aid thee, go.' And when I hear this Voice I have great joy. I would like always to hear it." But it is George Bernhard Shaw's play *Joan of Arc* that captures her style of prayer. He has Joan say, "How else can God speak to us except through...our imaginations."

As a film academic, I am fond of saying, "What you take to the screen can often destine what you take away from it." The desires and the bank of images within our imaginations can be potent forces for good when we come to encounter God and pray. As theologian Martin Borg says in *The God We Never Knew*, "Tell me your image of God and I will tell you your theology." That's why the Inquisition knew the imagination was such a dangerous thing.

There are so many images of God in the Old and New Testaments that entire books have been written on this topic. Some of our evangelical brothers and sisters have gone through the Bible and come up with a list of over 230 names or images that are used for God, which you can find at www.smilegodloves you.org/names.html.

For many Catholics, among the best impacts of Vatican II have been the many and varied biblical images of Father, Son, and Spirit that replaced that of the rather stern policeman and judge which many people had for a long time. Today some people in the Church either cannot understand the fear that motivated many people in their faith, or else they argue that it is overstated. My friend Margaret is a foil for both positions.

In 1952, Margaret was the night charge nurse for the operating theaters in a large Catholic public hospital. The nuns worked six a.m. to six p.m.; Margaret worked six p.m. to six a.m. On Wednesday, February 27, 1952, she came off her twelve-hour shift having raced from case to case for the entire night. She was dead on her feet and starving. On arrival home at her apartment, Margaret cooked herself up a large plate of bacon and eggs and devoured it. As she finished her breakfast, her roommate walked through the door sporting a big black cross on her forehead. Jane had just been to six-thirty a.m. Mass on Ash Wednesday. Margaret had just consumed bacon on a day of fast and abstinence. Convinced she was in a state of serious mortal sin and seized by panic, Margaret says she raced to the bathroom and tried to make herself vomit. When that wasn't successful, she very carefully caught the bus to St. Patrick's Church, which was where the first confessions in town started at eight a.m. Margaret was not then, and is not now, a religious nut or a Catholic zealot. She was a very normal Catholic for her time. "I thought that if I died before I could get to the confessional box, I would go to my final judgment and God would say, 'Look, Margaret, you have been a good Catholic, you've gone to Mass, said your prayers, and recited the Rosary. But what are we are going to do about the bacon? I'm sorry, my dear, the bacon is a deal breaker, off to hell for you for all eternity.' I really believed that. I know it sounds crazy now, but when I told my nursing friends what had happened later that day, they all thought I had done the right thing. No one thought I was mad."

Staying with this powerful and persuasive image, when we stand before God with the weakness and sinfulness of our own life, God will not settle old scores, take revenge, and exact retribution. Rather, God will be perfectly just and completely compassionate. How can I be so confident? Because that is the way Jesus acted with those he met, and this is the overwhelming picture he paints of his Father in heaven in the Gospels. Whatever image we find helpful in our prayer, we do not believe in a nasty God in heaven with the loving Jesus who came on earth and the emboldening Spirit who abides with us still. We believe that to have seen the Son is to have seen the Father and the Spirit. They are one God and act accordingly.

IMAGES OF GOD

I am always consoled that the most ancient image of Jesus used by the earliest Christians in their art was that of the Good Shepherd: a gentle, protective guide who seeks out and saves the lost one. When in the catacombs, where we might expect to find crucifixion scenes everywhere, we don't. We find Jesus as a young shepherd boy, holding the sheep on his shoulders leading her home. As powerful an image as Jesus on the cross is for us now, it was not until after Christianity became the imperial religion in the fourth century that images of the crucifixion became widespread. No doubt that image emerges so strongly at that time because the cross went from being a scandal, a folly, and a stumbling block (1 Cor. 1:1) to the sign of the one you crucified, now the emperor's God.

In the scriptures, we are given three different categories of images for God:

- That of a political leader—king, lawgiver, judge, and warrior;
- That of someone who is part of day-to-day life—a father, mother, potter, homemaker, doctor, shepherd, friend, lover, woman about to give birth, gardener, and healer; and
- That of nature where we find God in light, breath, a rock, the mountaintop, clouds, fire, or as a shield, bear, lion, or eagle.

At various times and stages of our lives different images will mean more to us than others. There are plenty to go around.

An image that has come to mean more to me in recent years is the Father, Son, and Spirit as homemakers. The image of God as homemaker is, sadly, not very developed in Christian spirituality, maybe because too many undomesticated men have had too much say for far too long! But this is an image that holds a lot for how and where we meet God in prayer. My old professor of liturgy used to say, "A priest who cannot host a dinner party should not preside at the Eucharist." You can see where this is going, and why. Jesus was good at dinner parties as host and guest. Meals mattered, and they still do.

In John's Gospel, Jesus says that as a result of our love for him and our fidelity to his word, the Father will come and make a home with us. The best homes are places where we relax because we are ourselves, we are known, and we know the others with whom we live. There is something intimate and familiar about our home that enables us to relax on many levels as we turn the key. Home is an earthy place where we don't get away with much and our vulnerability can be on display. A home, however, is more than a house in which people live. Homes need work and attention. A friend of mine says memories rarely "just happen," they need to be created. That sort of attention to a family's life turns a house into a home.

This is the world in which God enters our lives. God wants us to be relaxed and vulnerable in his presence. We don't need to put on a show or say what we think God wants to hear; that's a theater where we perform, not a home where we know each other. One element of our prayer is about being comfortable and intimate, about being who we are, rather than the persona we would prefer God to see. As with most of our homes, being at home with God has its ups and downs, days when we think we cannot bear to stay one more moment, other days where we could never imagine being anywhere else and then most days where we are neither up nor down and we just get on with the routine of our lives. What I find compelling about this image is that in prayer, God the homemaker seeks me out in the room where I have taken refuge that day and draws me out to enter the fray.

Without question, the most invoked image of God in prayer is as Father. We do it every time we say the Lord's Prayer. And so we should. For though it was not the only name Jesus used for God, and only one of the many images upon which he drew, it is a privileged name and image.

Biblical historians point out that Jesus was the first to apply the everyday word *abba* for God. *Daddy* in English is not a direct parallel word for *abba*, but it denotes the sort of relationship Jesus is invoking. Lost on us today, however, is that using that term would have been shocking in first-century Palestine—far too intimate, far too presumptuous—but it does indicate the sort of relationship Jesus had with the Father: the level of access, communion, affection, and ease. What is even more extraordinary, however, is that Jesus invites his followers to address God in a similar way, and so to enter into the same loving relationship. One of the strongest examples of Jesus using *abba* is also the most ancient, Mark 14:36. In the garden, Jesus cries out to God and says "abba" along with "father," so that first part of that verse could be translated "Daddy, Father, everything is possible for you...." This begins to reveal the break Jesus made with the images and language for God in prayer used before him. This is our legacy.

Not that "father" language is now value-neutral. Some people cannot say the Lord's Prayer as we have it, not because of what Jesus taught us to say, but because of what an earthly father did to them. Tragically, I know victims of clerical sexual abuse in the Catholic Church, where the priest is customarily called "Father," who have similar problems. In prayer, the father we are addressing, of course, is the very best possible, the most perfect imaginable father. Both sets of survivors know that God is not like their abusive father or priest, but it often takes time and healing for them to reclaim this ancient and important image for their prayer. Some people understandably struggle with this all their lives.

NAMES MATTER

Given that language is dynamic, however, our consciousness has been raised about the dominance in so much Christian private and public prayer of the masculine pronoun and masculine images. It doesn't worry some people, while for others it can be a great barrier. I think we should have an excellent inclusive language translation of the scriptures proclaimed at all public liturgy, since almost every scenario described or audience addressed therein involves both men and women. What we hear should be both a good translation of the text and a reflection of the context within which it was written and for whom. I am much more wary when it comes to horizontal or God language. For a while, I was of the opinion that removing the pronouns *him* and *his* for God and God's would do the trick. Having lived through that experiment, I have found it less than satisfactory. It often robs religious poetry of its immediacy, and takes away the personal relationship that our prayer is meant to reflect.

Rather than go the way of neutering God, maybe we should be more comfortable with using a variety of images for our public and private prayer. We noted earlier that one of the Bible's richest veins for images of God is in day-to-day situations: a father, mother, potter, homemaker, doctor, bridegroom, shepherd, friend, lover, woman about to give birth, gardener, and healer. Of this group, I would be very confident to assert that to call God our Mother or lover would cause the greatest difficulty.

God as lover does not have to be an erotic idea, although it certainly includes that. "God is Love" is, of course, one of the most important statements about God's nature in the New Testament. And there are enough images of God as a bridegroom coming to his wife for us not to exclude the idea that God can and does ravish us. As is well known by many, St. Teresa of Avila is the patron saint of a more earthy approach to prayer that takes eroticism seriously. Teresa described her relationship with Jesus: "It is a caressing of love so sweet which now takes place between the soul and God, that I pray God of His goodness to make him experience it who may think that I am lying." Teresa was famous for having ecstasies in her prayer.

God as Mother has been a much more contested image. While many people are comfortable enough imaging God to be like a woman giving birth, a woman losing a coin, baking some bread, or sweeping her house, praying to God as a mother is much more difficult. It should not be, for two reasons. First, if any name we give God does not capture God, then Father is not the absolutely last word on who God is. God is always greater than anything we can say or describe. Second, if God created mothers, which we do believe, and motherhood is a good thing, which it is, then motherhood must be part of God's nature. This is truer than most people think. Etymologically in the scriptures, the Hebrew root word for compassion, *rekhamim*, comes from the root word for womb, *rekhem*. So when we talk of God's compassion, which is everywhere in the Old and New Testaments and among God's greatest attributes, it a feminine and motherly image.

Not that advocacy for the motherhood of God always works out the way we expect. When I was a newly ordained deacon at Kings Cross, Sydney, in 1993, I had a wonderful pastor in a seventy-one-year-old Irish Jesuit priest called Donal Taylor. Fr. Donal never said "No" to any of my pastoral enthusiasms. He would simply say, "I'd be slow on that one"—which I was to discover was his way of saying, "No, don't do it!" On the Thursday before Trinity Sunday, while we were praying over the readings for the following weekend, and I was down to preach at all the Masses, he asked, "And what new spin is the young deacon going to put out on the ancient doctrine of the Trinity?" I told Donal that I was going to preach that while Father, Son, and Holy Spirit were privileged names for God in the Christian tradition, they did not exhaust the possibilities, and that God could helpfully be styled as our mother. Doubling over in the chair he said, "I'd be slow on that one."

Kings Cross is the red-light district of Sydney, and so the congregations there are a wonderful mixture of all God's children, some of them very colorful indeed. At the Vigil Mass, we had our usual parishioners, 120 young women who were boarders at St. Vincent's Catholic High School, and in the front pew was Con, the most famous homeless person in Kings Cross. As I advocated for the maternity of God, Con jumped up and expressed what was probably the majority position in the church: "God's not our mother! God's not our mother! Mary's our mother and God's our father!" Turning to Fr. Donal, he said, "Father Donal, this young bloke hasn't got a clue." Then he turned to the congregation and shouted, "And if you are listening to this bullshit, you need your head examined!" and marched out of the church. The congregation erupted with laughter and 120 young women thought this was the best Mass they had ever been to, so I looked at Donal, and then the congregation and said what could only be said in such a situation, "In the Name of the Father and the Son and the Holy Spirit. Amen," and sat down. And as I did, Donal turned to his unteachable deacon and mocked me. "I told you to be slow on that one."

Later, over dinner, Fr. Donal asked me, "Are you going to give the same homily tomorrow?" "I am not sure if you noticed," I replied, "but it did not go down well tonight." "Oh, you leave Con to me. He swore during Mass and I won't have it, so I will warn him off the place for a week. But I want you to give the same homily." "Really?" I replied. "Look, while God our Mother is not my cup of tea, there are those of us who need to hear that just because we name God as Father, it does not mean we have captured God or can control God." Fr. Donal has now seen God face to face, and I am sure she has welcomed him home with compassion and love.

Why bother praying? Because we have been given both a vivid imagination and a vast array of biblical images to get us started. For whatever image or word we use, God is always more than we can ever say; but that does not mean our names are unimportant, for our image of God reveals our personal theology as well.

Chapter 3

What Is Distinctive about Christian Prayer?

In the introduction I said that the most energetic feedback I received in regard to *Where the Hell Is God?* was in relation to what I said about intercessory prayer. In that book, I said that the most common form of address from humanity to God is asking for something to happen to someone somewhere. I argued that all the sacrifices and prayers in the world cannot change God because we believe God is unchanging. That is a rock-solid part of classical theology: God's immutability.

So what does our petitionary prayer do? Why bother praying to a God who does not change? When we pray we are asking our holy, loving, and unchanging God to change us, and thereby change the world. I went on to say that the way I see and hear some Christians talk about their prayer convinced me that a good number of Christians do not actually pray to the God and Father of Jesus Christ, but to Zeus.

Zeus was the king of all the Greek gods and was in charge of the skies and thunder, and so was Olympus' resident meteorologist. A good friend of mine who is also a distinguished writer and a classicist challenged me over the way I portrayed the interaction between Zeus and mortals in *Where the Hell Is God?* He pointed out several passages in the ancient texts where Zeus is mocked and challenged. So it was not as simple as the reward/punishment relationship I had portrayed. Still, it is true that in the traditional presentation of Zeus in Greek mythology he is not an easy god with whom to get along. Though he could be loving and kind, he was more famous for being moody and unpredictable. When his ire was raised he killed, maimed, punished, and handed other gods and mortals over to be tortured in a variety of exotic ways. Life with Zeus was unpredictable.

As with all the Greek gods, penance, prayer, and sacrifice were the usual offerings. In Zeus' case, however, slaughtered oxen, which were then an enormous economic unit, were offered. The hierarchy of sacrifices and the length of prayers seem to have been in relation to how much a petitioner wanted Zeus to listen to the plea, change his mind, or be kind to him or her.

Rightly, since the earliest centuries of the Church, our God was different from the gods that had gone before, including Zeus. For us, God cannot wake up in a bad mood today, and he is not unpredictable. It is nearly impossible to have a steady and loving relationship with a volatile human being, so how much more fraught would our relationship with God be if he were characterized by being random (in the classic sense of the word) or erratic? Jesus, the Word of the Father for the world, was strong and constant. And, on the nature of God, the Apostle James says, "Every good and perfect gift is from above, coming down from the Father of the heavenly lights, who does not change like shifting shadows" (Jas 1:17).

If our experience and image of God is crucial to how we pray, then I have seen some Christians speak of and promote a God who is more of the stereotype of Zeus than of the God and Father of Jesus Christ. Think of some of the things people shared with me about their take on why intercessory prayer is not answered:

"Not enough people must have been praying for that intention."

"We have not prayed long enough or hard enough for God to hear us."

"God is testing us even by not answering our prayer to
  see how much we love him."
And most revealingly of all, "unless you do penance as
  well as pray, then God will not answer your prayers
  because you are not serious."

So this take on God and prayer is alive and well, and very sincerely held by good people. I also know that others do not
bother praying because they reject this model of prayer—and
the God that goes with it.

I like the story of the petitioner who calls heaven and
encounters one of those dreadful electronic directories.

"Thank you for calling Heaven. Please select one of
  the following options:
    Press 1 for Requests;
    Press 2 for Thanksgiving;
    Press 3 for Complaints;
    Press 4 for All other personal inquires;
    Press 5 for Information on the whereabouts of
        deceased family and friends;
    Press 6 for Your heavenly reservation.
  Heaven is closed for the Jewish, Christian, and
  Muslim Holy Days; please pray again on Monday
  morning at 8:30 am. If you need emergency assis-
  tance when this office is closed, contact your local
  priest, rabbi, or imam."

Then, while waiting, we would hear on a never-ending loop,
King David sing a Psalm, Mary sing the Magnificat, or Miriam
belt out her Red Sea hit with the original tambourine accompa-
niment. Every twenty seconds a familiar voice would cut back
in, "I'm sorry, Heaven is busy helping other sinners right now.

However, your prayer is important to us and will be answered in the order it was received, so please stay on the line."

After fifteen minutes the voice would say, "Our computers show that you have already prayed three times today. Please hang up and try again tomorrow."

This tongue-in-cheek presentation makes two serious points. I think one of the reasons people don't bother praying is that they usually equate praying with petitionary prayer, asking for something. Second, when they feel they have been put on hold by God, or turned down several times, they disconnect the line. Prayer isn't worth the trouble because either no one is there, or whoever is there doesn't seem to care.

But it doesn't have to be like this. If we need rich and varied images for God for our prayer, we also need many ways of praying. We don't have to invent these; they are already in the scriptures and in our tradition. All we need to do is remind ourselves of them, maybe be introduced to them, and adapt them for the here and now. Christian prayer has followed the categories of the psalms. Here and elsewhere, I have already dealt with my take on petitionary prayer, but there are five other categories:

- Praise and thanksgiving;
- Lamentation, crying out in anguish;
- Affirming our trust and faith;
- Singing of our salvation;
- And simply waiting upon the presence of God.

PRAISE AND THANKSGIVING

In the *Sacramentary*—as the first and second editions of the Missal were called—the Preface of Weekdays in Ordinary Time IV reads:

You have no need of our praise,
yet our desire to thank You is itself Your gift.
Our prayer of thanksgiving adds nothing to Your
    greatness,
but makes us grow in Your grace,
through Jesus Christ our Lord.

I used to love saying those lines at the Eucharist (sadly, I think this older translation is preferable to what we now have in the third edition of the *Roman Missal*). The gratitude we have for God is a gift we receive to recognize the gift and the giver and be filled with praise and thanksgiving. I hope nearly everyone has had those overwhelming moments of gratitude, those instances of euphoric praise. They can be the times when we feel most alive: giving birth to a child, getting married or professing vows as a religious or being ordained, doing well in studies, attaining a degree, beholding natural beauty, getting a job, or clinching a deal. The events that bring out our praise and thanksgiving are very revealing of our values and priorities.

Naturally, we are grateful for different things as we get older. Since my sister's car accident, which rendered her a quadriplegic, I am especially grateful for the seemingly small things of everyday life, the earthy things I can do but she cannot. Don't say this book isn't practical—if you have never sat on the toilet and been filled with praise and thanksgiving because you can go all on your own, then your prayer life is about to become a lot richer. The old line goes, "you don't know what you've got till it's gone." I often turn the smallest room in the house into a house of prayer.

I do a lot of work with teachers, and one of the things that has struck me in recent years is how many of them say, "The two fastest disappearing words in the English language are 'please' and 'thank you' because these days kids think everything is a right." We should not only blame parents and their children for this. Have you noticed that common courtesy is on the wane; that some adults seem to be angrily demanding of everyone around them? I am sometimes embarrassed at how they speak to those who are serving us. Good customer service should not come because I yell louder than everyone else does. We are better than that.

The reality is that we all need to cultivate a habit of saying "please" and "thank you," not just because it is a sign of civil society, but because it enables us to recognize that each person has human dignity and deserves our respect, even if they are being paid to do their job. It helps create a world in which people are never mistaken for commodities.

It is not by accident that praise and thanksgiving are linked in the psalms. The people I know who are most grateful are also the most generous when it comes to praising others. And often the people we find it hardest to praise are the ones to whom we are closest, our wife or husband, children, friends, parents, or fellow members of religious communities. We don't have to be stingy with praise; there will always be enough to go around. We just have to make sure it is sincere. There are those who worry that these days, when no child can fail and everyone wins a prize, our children are not emotionally robust enough to suffer the disappointments of life. There is something in that, but we don't have to withhold praise from one another; we just have to find opportunities to celebrate truly and authentically what we can.

If we are full of praise and gratitude for the daily things and the people that enrich our lives, then larger moments of recognition and appreciation take care of themselves. A good place to start is to write down all the things for which you are grateful. It does not matter how small or seemingly stupid they are. It's your list. In compiling that list you are already praying because an ancient cornerstone of prayer is that our desire to thank God is itself God's gift. Be grateful.

LAMENTATION, CRYING OUT IN ANGUISH

When I was advocating that we should not pray for rain, I went on to suggest that rather than gathering for a Mass to ask God to open the heavens, we should gather in a church for a liturgical lament, a collective expression of communal pain, crying to God about how we are experiencing our present life and inviting God into the griefs and anxieties of the moment. In Catholic liturgy we have lost the power of lamentation. The psalmists had no such problem. They cried, they screamed, they demanded, and they railed against God over their pain. By comparison our liturgical behavior is very tame indeed, at least in the Christian West.

Have you ever been to a Greek Orthodox funeral, especially when the circumstances are especially tragic? I once attended the funeral of a friend's wife who committed suicide. She was suffering from postpartum depression. The behavior during the liturgy in the church was almost the same as I would expect in the Catholic Church. Everyone was clearly upset. When we came outside, however, and especially when we went for the Rite of Burial, it was a very different scene. It was not just the stereotype of the Greek women draped in black wanting to hurl themselves into the grave; there can be a theatricality to that scenario. The burial I attended was not scripted. It was permitted and understood. It was the husband, father, mother, and most of the family who yelled and screamed and beat the ground with anguish and grief. It was such a complex mixture of loss and regret, of anger at her taking her own life, and of human helplessness.

My response was curious, at least to me. At first, I wanted to run a mile. Some of my other friends did just that. This was too tribal, too primal. But the longer I stayed, the more I came to see this lament was the perfect response to this most tragic of days. I think it was the sanest funeral I have ever attended. I use that verb carefully. There is, of course, good research to show that when people are allowed to grieve publicly and powerfully, it helps them recover from their trauma more quickly. Public lamentation is always culturally specific, but as the outpouring of grief over the death of Diana, Princess of Wales, showed us, maybe things are changing for the better in the West.

I suspect the reality is very different in private. There, in our spiritual or physical rooms, I think some of us have no trouble lamenting our situation. Not that everyone can. Many people have told me that while they would like to yell at God, they cannot. I remind them that of the 150 psalms we have, sixty-five are categorized as cries of lament, anger, protest, despair, and complaint. I send them off to pray over Psalm 88, the darkest of all the psalms, and then encourage them to then go on to Psalms 3, 12, 22, 44, 57, 80, and 139. Not that I share in any way the belief in some of these psalms that God has sent the misfortune in an active way, but I am in awe of the way the psalmist unloads on God. It is consoling and terrific. Such confidence.

One of the most moving, private lamentations was also one of the most public. It was fictional. In "Two Cathedrals," the forty-fourth episode of *West Wing*, President Bartlett has attended the funeral of his beloved private secretary. Mrs. Landingham was hit by a drunk driver on the day of her retirement from the White House. As the congregation disperses from her funeral at the National Cathedral in Washington, DC, the President asks to be left alone. Actor Martin Sheen then delivers some of the finest moments I have ever seen on television. He turns to God and laments.

> …You're a son of a bitch, you know that?… "You can't conceive, nor can I, the appalling strangeness of the mercy of God," says Graham Greene. I don't know whose ass he was kissin' there, 'cause I think you're just vindictive….What did I ever do to you but praise

his glory and praise his name? ...I've committed many sins. Have I displeased you, you feckless thug?... Am I really to believe that these are the acts of a loving God? A just God? A wise God? To hell with your punishments. I was your servant here on Earth. And I spread your word and I did your work. To hell with your punishments. To hell with you.

It is no surprise to me that this episode of *West Wing* is considered by many critics to be the best of the 156 installments that were made in that fine series.

Apart from the President's understandable but dubious theology, God has big shoulders. Later in the same episode, Mrs. Landingham appears to the President and knowingly and rightly says, "God doesn't make cars crash, and you know it. Stop using me as an excuse." He understands our lamentations because he knows the anguish in our hearts. I think God lives by the generally sensible advice: *better out than in*. We should all bother him a lot more with all our lamentations. God can take it.

AFFIRMING OUR TRUST AND FAITH IN GOD

For most of us, the actions demanded by the "St. Jude, hope of the hopeless, prayer guides" are not taken all that seriously. We do not attend to the instructions of these dreadful chain letters because they reduce God to being an unpredictable tyrant: "I will do what you want only if you jump through these hoops." It is the opposite of trusting in God. For the record, we do not have to write out a prayer nine times and leave it in nine churches for God to listen to us, or for him to take our prayers seriously. Still, St. Jude's patronage does exercise a power in the modern imagination because there are many more people living desperate lives in our community than we could credit. Trust me! St. Jude won't mind, rip up the chain letters (and anything else like them). It is Jesus, not Jude, who is the hope of the hopeless, and he does not ask us to jump through hoops to get our prayer heard and answered. He asks us to trust him.

There has been a lot of research about how one person trusts another. It all hinges on being vulnerable to the other. This is a bit easier when it is between human beings: we can see each other. We cannot see God, only feel and encounter him, so being vulnerable to God is not easy. To accomplish it we need that most subtle of gifts, true humility. The word *humility* comes from the Latin word *humus,* meaning "earth." If we want our prayer to be about trusting God, then we have to stop trying to be the creator and be the creature. An Alcoholics Anonymous slogan sums it up nicely: *Let go and let God.*

Other things that assist us to trust are the mutuality of the relationship, when both parties are prepared to take appropriate personal risks, and an inability to control the other person. In each case, we can see how this works out in our relationship with God. Out of love, God gave us life and invites us, rather than coerces us, to respond to that gift in a mutual exchange. God has taken great risks in creating the world and giving us free will, and with St. Paul we can affirm that he risked everything in taking flesh of our flesh in Jesus, and offering us salvation. Even still, when we enter into a relationship with Christ, he enables us to take the risk of not living half a life, but realizing our full potential and living life to the fullest. While some think trusting God means we have to become God's marionettes, the relationship we are invited into is much more about mutuality and respect. It has long been accepted in philosophy that God treats us like adults, that we are not God's playthings. In fact, the opposite is true. In giving us free will, God does not want to control us, but waits patiently, inviting us, alluring us into the life of grace.

The Jesuits and Dominicans have been fighting about who controls whom and for what reason since 1588. It is called the debate over free will and grace, and it is illustrated by one question: "Could Mary have said 'No!' to the angel?" The Jesuit position was yes: Mary could have said no to the angel, but what makes her yes richer and stronger is that she was given human freedom. The Dominican position was no: such was the grace of the Immaculate Conception that Mary had to say yes to the angel. In 1582, Pope Clement VIII said you are both right, now shut up. And, of course, the Jesuits are right!

Our freedom before God means that the will of God is discovered on the larger canvas rather than in the details. God wants us to live out the theological virtues of faith, hope, and love (1 Cor 13), and to embody in all we do the fruits of the Spirit: love, joy, peace, patience, kindness, goodness, faithfulness, gentleness, and self-control (Gal 5:22). By trusting in the Lord, which is neither simple nor easy, we discover there is not a heavenly blueprint, as such, for our life. We find, however, that through the blessing of time and place, the gifts of nature and grace, we trust God to enable us to realize our potential in the greatest way possible, even if that involves having to do things that are difficult, demanding, and sacrificial. This response is not out of fear and compulsion, but comes from love and desire.

If we have the humility to let go and let God, it does not mean that God does all the work. It means that in our prayer God treats us as adult, in a mutual relationship where, with God we are invited to risk things, maybe everything.

Trust in God is often about being vulnerable to God through the seemingly ordinary events of life, and responding in the most generous, good, and loving way possible.

SINGING OF OUR SALVATION

A friend of mine is a great lover of classical music. His knowledge of it is vast. He only needs to hear a few bars of most musical works and he confidently declares, "Mozart's Piano Concerto in A" or "Stravinsky's *Rite of Spring*." He's always right. Another of his superfluous but amusing gifts is to pick the singer. He can hear a soprano and declare it to be Callas, Norman, Te Kanawa, or Sutherland. He always knows which of the Three Tenors is belting out that particular top C. What intrigues me about this gift is that he remembers the timbres of each voice, not just the famous ones, but some rather obscure soloists as well. It helps that he has listened to the sounds of these voices for years.

It's the same with recognizing the voice of Christ—it comes with practice and exposure to it. That's why we pray. The repetition of prayer isn't just about doing the same dumb things over and over. It is the practice we need to attune our hearing, to listen to the sound of God's voice so that even if it is faintly heard amidst the din, we pick it out, lift our head, turn our gaze, and walk toward it. These days there are a multitude of voices clamoring for our attention, and the loudest or the longest ones are often not the wisest ones. There are a lot of songs to sing. We need practice at listening, hearing, attuning our ears, and adding harmony.

The psalms are replete with invitations to sing of our salvation. Psalm 95, 118, 62, 20, and 13 are just a few of them. Singing in some cultures is a very tame affair, especially in church. In the United Kingdom they can sing great old hymns at church and at their other sacred space—the football stadium. The United States is admiringly enthusiastic about singing inside and outside the church. They sing with gusto. The Italians will sing everywhere except at Mass. The Irish don't even get a chance to have a go. By mutual consent it seems to me, many of their Sunday Masses have no music at all—"get 'em in and get 'em out" appears to be the motto. Australians are coy about singing anywhere, save the shower or when we have had too much to drink. Many of us don't even know the words to our National Anthem! So when it comes to Mass, it is a rare congregation down under that will lift the roof. But we are all called to sing of our salvation as a way of praying.

Music in church is not there to annoy the tone deaf. It is theology set to music. That's why we should be very careful about what we sing. The words and the music matter because, sixty years on, most people do not remember verbatim what they learned in a religious education class, but they often recall a hymn or spiritual song, sometimes in its entirety. Singing commits things to memory in a way that the words on their own do not.

Maybe it is that this traditional category of prayer is not actually about singing, as good as I think that is, but is a metaphor about words and memory. One of the finest themes that emerges out of the Old and New Testaments is of remembrance. The Jews are constantly told to commit this to memory, not to forget what God has done, and to keep calling it to mind. Jesus says to celebrate the Eucharist "in memory of me," and even the good thief simply asks Jesus to "remember me" when he comes into his kingdom. The word *remember* comes from the Latin *rememorari*; meanng "again" and "be mindful of"; literally "recall to mind." The reason we are constantly told to remember is, as poet and philosopher George Santayana said in *Life of Reason, Reason in Common Sense*, "Those who cannot remember the past are condemned to repeat it."

Taking the Bible as seriously as we should, the worst thing to forget is what God has already done for us. We have been saved in Jesus Christ the Lord. We don't save ourselves. We cannot earn salvation by good works, prayers, or penance. They are the responses we make to the salvation of Christ that we claim here and now.

And how we live is the way by which those we love will find the gift of God's salvation for themselves. Now, we all know we are works in progress. We may well be saved by Christ, but it is quite another thing to accept that gift, claim it, nurture it, and live it in our daily lives. We can freely reject it. Some do so every time it's offered. We sing of God's salvation so that we remember not only what help has been given in ages past, but what help and companionship is available from God right now.

We also sing about what will be in the future. To learn this saving song, to sing it well, to understand its nuances and possibilities, we need practice and repetitions so that at the moment of our death, in the midst of all the other sounds as we leave this world, we will hear Christ's voice—soothing, reassuring, comforting, and confident. It's our prayer that as we hear God's merciful and loving song, we will do what we have tried to do throughout our lives—recognize it clearly, savor it, walk straight toward it, and join in the chorus—because they will be singing our song.

WAITING UPON THE PRESENCE OF GOD

Have you ever noticed how versatile the word *waiting* is? There is such a variety of ways in which we use it: to wait in line; what are you waiting for?; to keep someone waiting; wait a minute!; let's wait and see; to wait on a table and to wait for a table; to wait your turn; waiting in the wings; waiting to happen; something will have to wait; just wait until...; there's no time to wait; when something can or cannot wait.

In the scriptures we are called "to wait upon the Lord" 106 times. Psalms 25, 27, 37, 52, 62, 104, 106, and 130 all call us to wait, in the sense of being patient. You can't rush God. Using the modern vernacular, this means that some part of our prayer life should be about "chilling out." Earlier I confessed to being an extrovert. I find that keeping a straight back, controlling my breathing, and sitting still for what seems an eternity is not my natural suit. But learning to be comfortable with that style of prayer has been one of the great gifts of my spiritual pilgrimage. Mind you, in my case it has taken an unusual turn. I personally find it easier to meditate flat on my back, often on my bed. This would be deadly for other people, especially first thing in the morning or after lunch. It would be straight back to sleep for most others. In this posture, however, I rarely fall off to sleep, and if I do, I assume I need the sleep. Even though Jesus tells people to rise up from their bed, what I have discovered by trial and error is that my extroverted brain needs to be prompted to settle and be still. Lying down on my bed tells me to chill out, far more than sitting up straight in a chair does. From my bed, I wait upon the Lord.

Like many other meditators, I find my brain sometimes goes a hundred miles an hour. So another technique I have learned is to use my rosary beads (more on the prayer itself later) as simple prayer beads and just pick up a short phrase out of the scripture passage upon which I am praying, or a line that sums up how I am before God that day, or a theme in the liturgical season, and then I repeat it as I pass the beads slowly through my fingers. Not only does this help me come to the quiet and gives me something tangible to hold and use, it links me to an ancient practice in the Church, and beyond us to Islamic and Buddhist traditions as well. When my mind empties, I find myself waiting not just *on* the Lord, but *with* the Lord. "Be still and know that I am God" (Ps 46:10).

This idea of waiting in our prayer can be seen as being passive, but it can also be a very active business indeed. In Hebrew, the word for *wait* is *qavah*, which means "to bind together into a cord." It comes from people understanding that while a piece of string might be strong, when you bind the strings together into a rope it can be immeasurably stronger and more workable. So when we wait upon the Lord in prayer it can be about harnessing our resources, doing a stress test, and making sure that all our energies are pulling together in the same direction in loving and serving the Lord each day.

The most common way we think about waiting upon the Lord, however, is when we are anxious. Think of people waiting in hospital corridors for news of a sick relative, or a parent who stays up with an infant who may be teething or has a high temperature. Some sit by the phone waiting to be reassured that a loved one is safe and well, or that we have passed the exam, or got the job. Many of us experienced sitting in a doctor's waiting room for a test result. Many of these are highly stressful occasions. These can be hardest moments in which to pray. But we have a great patron saint in Simeon, the old man who waited and waited because he believed the Lord's promise that he would not see death without seeing the Messiah. This tender story is stunning just as it is, but giving it a more psychological reading, we can see that some things cannot and will not go in peace until their time has come. We can't force them. If earlier I said we cannot save ourselves, then as difficult as it is to hear, it is equally true that we cannot save anyone else. That includes our children, spouse, grandchildren, parents, or friends. Sometimes we bother praying because there is nothing else we can do. We don't have to get the words right or even know the details of how we want something to develop, we just want the one we love to be at peace, made well, freed from fear, and to be more faithful, hopeful, or loving. My favorite verse at times like this is Romans 8:26, "The Spirit helps us in our weakness; for we do not know how to pray as we ought, but that very Spirit intercedes with sighs too deep for words."

After my sister's car accident, I visited this moment many times: no words; no great ideas; numbness, powerlessness; sighs.

It was when this pain was most acute for me that I started lighting candles in churches again. I thought I had left that pious practice behind in childhood. How wrong I was. As much as I understand the fire codes that govern churches' insurance policies these days, I feel let down when a church does not have a shrine at which I can light a candle. I also resent those flickering electric utilitarian contraptions. They have no poetry about them. Rather, in a time of anxiety when we are waiting for a better dawn in regard to a particular dark night, there is nothing as satisfying as taking a small candle, lighting it, seeing it among scores if not hundreds of others, and leaving it there with my prayer as we all wait upon the Lord.

A particularly Catholic prayer practice that is all about waiting upon the Lord and has made a recent return, especially among some young adults, is the Adoration of the Blessed Sacrament. Having a central focus or image for meditation and contemplation is attested to in nearly every religious tradition in the world. But for Catholics the consecrated host is not simply a focus for prayer. In his document *Transiturus* of 1264, establishing the feast of the Body of Christ, Pope Urban IV spoke to the wonder and strangeness of the mystery, "the giver comes in the gift." The celebration of the Eucharist, from which the consecrated host comes, is the giver in the gift, transforming us into himself not simply as sign and proof of love, but that love made real and available to us in our daily lives.

Adoration has a complex history and arose when the vast majority of Catholics only infrequently received Holy Communion at the Eucharist. We know that some people ascribed to the host magical properties, while for others the adoration of the Blessed Sacrament took the place of celebrating the Eucharist. We still need to be alert to these extremes even now. Our prayer before the monstrance should lead us back to its summit and source. In fact, as St. Augustine says, the best devotion to the

Eucharist, inside or outside the action of the Mass, should lead us to acclaim, "O mystery of goodness! O sign of unity! O bond of charity!" In other words, praying by using this long and venerable practice should lead us to contemplate God's unconditional love for us in Christ, work for unity in the Church among Christians and in the world, and become more loving.

Why bother praying? It does not matter if we have developed bad habits in limiting prayer to only asking for things, but prayer is much, much richer than that. By all means let's keep asking God to keep changing us, but let's also give praise and thanksgiving; cry out in lamentation; affirm our trust and faith; sing of our salvation; and simply wait upon the Lord. There is a way to pray for all seasons under the sun.

Chapter 4

Schools of Prayer

If the biblical tradition has given us multiple ways to communicate with God, then the lived tradition of the Church has expanded these into what are grandly called schools of prayer. Don't let anyone ever tell you that there is one way to God, one way of praying in private or public. The scriptures and the tradition of the Church tell a very different story. In every era of the Christian Church's life, many charismatic individuals have emerged to challenge the Church in its practices, in its discipline or lack of it, and often in the way we pray. No matter how much the Christians of their day did not like what they heard at the time, history has seen many of these individuals declared saints, which is more than we can say for their poor detractors. Around holy men and women schools of spirituality developed, either in their lifetimes, or subsequently. There are scores of these schools, but for brevity here I want to concentrate on the six longest-lived and most popular: Desert, Benedictine, Franciscan, Dominican, Carmelite, and Ignatian. There are also libraries written on and around each of them, but this sampling is how we might start to realize how many rooms there actually are in the Father's spiritual house.

DESERT SPIRITUALITY

From the third to the fifth centuries people left the towns and cities in what is today called the Middle East, and moved into the harsh deserts to pray. Initially St. Antony of Egypt and his earliest companions were hermits, but communities developed and a common way of life and prayer emerged. It was the beginning of monastic life, though most of the desert communities maintained a hermetical lifestyle and came together once a week for the Eucharist, prayer, and conversation. They were great scholars too, and left behind them a wealth of literature. St. Antony the Great, St. Macarius the Great, St. Arsenius, St. Paul the Hermit, St. John the Dwarf, St. Mary of Egypt, Amma Syncletica, and many others were inspired by Jesus' forty days in the desert and the example of John the Baptist.

The spirituality that emerges is marked by a withdrawal from the vanities of the world to first find God, and then find oneself before God. It is told that a young monk went to the elder desert father, Abba Moses, to ask where he would find most enlightenment, "…and the old man said, 'Go and sit in your cell and your cell will teach you everything.'" It was in the figurative and physical desert cell that the desert fathers and mothers came to value humility, fear of the Lord, the purification of desires, and freedom from individualism through self-knowledge and asceticism.

Sometimes it is understandably criticized for being overly harsh and world hating. There is something in this commentary, but it can be exaggerated. St. Antony was very careful about the centrality of moderation, and if the writings of the desert fathers and mothers are to be believed, they lived with a joy and vitality that many would envy. I like the story about a monk who went to Abba Poemen and asked him, "When we see brothers who are falling asleep during the services, should we arouse them so that they will be watchful?" Poemen said, "For my part, when I see a brother falling asleep, I place his head on my knees and let him rest."

When we look at how the journey to the desert is used in the Bible, it is filled with a mixture of pleasure and pain, abundant with revelation, transformation, and recreation. As we find in Jesus' example in the desert, we do not believe that the desert is only about loss, but it can be a path through which we emerge recreated, richer for the experience.

For many of us who might yearn for the experience, it is not practical to retreat to a physical desert. But one of the desert mothers, Amma Syncletica, wrote, "There are many who live in the mountains and behave as if they were in the town, and they are wasting their time. It is possible to be a solitary in one's mind while living in a crowd, and it is possible for one who is a solitary to live in the crowd of his own thoughts."

Desert spirituality reminds those of us who live in towns and cities in our own particular deserts, that temptation is not sin. To be tempted by something is not the same as doing it. Temptations are the allures that make destructive choices look good. In one sense, the bad news is that we know from the lives of the saints, especially the desert fathers and mothers, that the closer we get to God, the more temptations increase. The good news is that we can learn how to deal with them. Usually, temptations have a context and a history. They can come when we are feeling most deserted and vulnerable, and they normally strike us at the weakest points in our character. To deal with them we need to be aware of their pattern, the way they con us into believing that the destructive behavior is "not that bad," will be "just this once," or even "for the last time." It also helps if we are aware of the danger signs in our lives that can weaken our defenses. Tiredness and boredom are two telltale signs of which to be aware. We are both attacked at the most vulnerable parts of ourselves, and allured by what some call the narcotics of modern living. I love the word *narcotic* in this context; it comes from the Greek word *narkō* meaning "to numb," or "to numb the pain." Today we use a whole series of things to deaden the pain of modern living: drugs, alcohol, sex, food, work, gambling, technology, and shopping. If you just scored six out of eight you're in trouble! These things can be used for good and necessary purposes, but they can sometimes become narcotics. They do not take away the pain of living but temporarily mask its effects. Sometimes we all need to venture with Christ into the desert and confront these temptations head-on. Occasionally we need to do it physically if we can separate ourselves for a while so we are more humble and respectful of the Lord, purify our desires, get free from individualism through self-knowledge, and be ascetical in as much as it draws us closer to God. The beauty of this movement is summed up by Amma Syncletica: "In the beginning there is struggle and a lot of work for those who come near to God. But after that, there is indescribable joy. It is just like building a fire: at first, it is smoky and your eyes water, but later you get the desired result. Thus we ought to light the divine fire in ourselves with tears and effort."

BENEDICTINE SPIRITUALITY

Although it bears his name, St. Benedict did not found the Benedictine Order, but a movement that has grown into the Benedictine family. He and his sister Scholastica both founded a monastery and a convent respectively. Benedict wrote a rule for his community, which he seemed to have intuited could be lived elsewhere, by women and men equally. If there is one thing that characterizes Benedict's rule it is structure, but not as an end in itself. The Rule's break-up of the day into periods for liturgy, community life, meals, reading, and work were so the monk or nun could come closer to God. He understood that without structure some of us go adrift.

The rigor of Benedictine monasteries was not easy, but Benedict's rule is marked by its gentle tone and compassion. He was clearly reacting to some of the excessive asceticism that had gone before him. The whole point of the Rule was "to establish a school for the Lord's service" (*Prolog* 45) where "we progress in this way of life [that, in his love, God shows us] and in faith," and so "run along the way of God's commandments, our hearts overflowing with the inexpressible delight of love" so that "never swerving from his instructions, but faithfully observing his teaching in the monastery until death, we shall through patience share in the passion of Christ that we may deserve also to share in his Kingdom" (*Prolog* 21; 49–50).

Although he makes provision for monks and nuns to live as hermits for a period, he was a genius in trying to work out how people can live together in close quarters for their whole adult lives. He discovered through trial and error that silence in the day was as important as conversation, that prayer and work and learning were essential, as was staying put, and that everyone had to contribute to the best of their abilities and gifts. Benedictine monasteries went on to be some of the greatest halls of learning in medieval Europe. St. Benedict even rejected the idea of the tyrannical abbot or abbess. He was into consultative government long before it was fashionable. "Whenever any important matters have to be settled in the monastery, the abbot should call together the whole community and himself explain what is to be discussed. After he has heard the brethren's advice, he should reflect upon it, and then do what he judges best. Now, the reason for our saying that all should be summoned for counsel is that the Lord often reveals what is better to a younger person."

Often many people quote the opening word of St. Benedict's Rule, *obsculta*, as "Listen." Before we could obey the Rule, Benedict knew we would have to listen. Obedience is not about jumping to commands, but it starts with everyone listening to one another and to God. That is a rich idea. The first sentence of the Rule of St. Benedict is a quote from Proverbs 4:20: "Listen carefully, my child, to your master's precepts, and incline the ear of your heart." What is extraordinary about this opening line of a monastic rule is that the monk or nun is called firstly to listen to God, not the abbot, not the community, and not even the Rule, but listen to discern what God is saying to his or her heart. This matters. For all of Benedict's attention to the minutiae of day-to-day living, he never lost the big picture. True spirituality is not about keeping rules and laws. It is about discernment of what God is doing in one's heart. As we saw above, St. Benedict believed that the youngest member of the community might be the holiest and the wisest.

For us today who have no need or desire to join a Benedictine monastery, this school of spirituality going back to the sixth century has plenty to teach us about many things to do with how we pray and how our lives affect our prayer. Most of us need a structure to function well and to be productive. Problems arise when we do not know what we are doing or why. So we need a rhythm of life that keeps a clear focus on the positive outcome of coming closer to the Father, Son, and Holy Spirit. It means developing productive patterns for work, rest, learning, and play, so that when we are tempted to walk away we have good habits upon which to rely.

I think Benedict's emphasis on rest and sleep is very important. Think about how you answer the question, "How are you?" Most people will say either, "I'm exhausted!" or "I'm run off my feet!" How do we know that's correct? When was the last time you asked someone, "How are you?" and they said, "I've got the life/work balance perfectly in order, thanks for asking." These days most people seem frantic or exhausted. There is now a competition to see who is the most frantic and who is the most exhausted. A culture of exhaustion militates against a good prayer life, because we are just too tired.

At its most fundamental, Benedictine spirituality is all about appropriate boundaries and moderation, not so that we become lifeless and joyless, but so that we pace ourselves and develop the range of gifts we have. These gifts, however, are not meant just for us, but for the wider community, and in that regard nothing is too small, no act of kindness and service too inconsequential. St. Benedict says that because everyday items serve the community and enliven it, they should be treated with the same respect as the sacred vessels. Here is a man who understood the link between liturgy and life.

Because St. Benedict thought living life at a less breakneck speed was sane, he was passionate about savoring things—actions, food, creation, people, and especially words. His *lectio divina*, a style of mindful reading and savoring, is practiced by many people in all walks of life. We can often miss important things because we are not deliberate enough about the details. Integrating the parts of the day into a whole is a gift St. Benedict gave us. In *The Rule of Benedict: Insights for the Ages*, Joan Chittister, OSB, says, "To those who think for a moment that the spiritual life is an excuse to ignore the things of the world, to go through time suspended above the mundane...let this chapter be fair warning. Benedictine spirituality is as much about good order, wise management, and housecleaning as it is about the meditative and the immaterial dimensions of life. Benedictine spirituality sees the care of the earth and the integration of prayer and work, body and soul, as essential parts of the journey to wholeness that answers the emptiness in each of us."

Finally, if we want to be obedient, we all better start listening very carefully. In this regard, I enjoy the story of Fr. Browne. It may not come as a surprise to some readers to learn that one of the few people to get off the *Titanic* before it set sail across the Atlantic Ocean was a Jesuit Priest. Irish Jesuit Frank Browne finished his theological studies in 1912. As an ordination gift, his uncle Robert Browne, the independently wealthy Bishop of Cloyne, sent him a first-class ticket for the maiden voyage of the *Titanic* from Southampton in the UK to Cherbourg in France and then to Queenstown (now Cobh) in Cork. While on board, a wealthy American Catholic family befriended the thirty-two-year-old priest and offered to pay his fare all the way to New York and back to Ireland. He went to the now-famous Marconi room and sent a telegram to his Provincial Superior in Dublin asking for permission to accept the offer. Fr. Browne spent his time on board taking over a thousand images of the working ship. When the *Titanic* reached Cork Harbor there was a telegram waiting for Frank Browne from his superior. It read: "GET OFF THAT SHIP. PROVINCIAL." Browne was one of eight passengers to disembark in Ireland and he took the last known photographs of the *Titanic* as it disappeared on the Atlantic horizon, broken-hearted that he was not on board. His thousand photographs were the only ones to survive the crossing and document the workings of *Titanic's* tragic maiden and final voyage. Fr. Browne carried that telegram in his coat pocket until the day he died in 1960. He was fond of holding it aloft in his sermons and lectures saying, "This telegram proves that Holy Obedience can save a man's life." If we want to be obedient, then we had better become good listeners.

FRANCISCAN SPIRITUALITY

Nearly every major movement of spirituality in Christianity has arisen to answer a set of serious issues in the life of the Church. No other school of prayer proves this more than the Franciscans. The Church of the late eleventh and twelfth centuries was split in many directions. The Holy Roman Empire and the Papal States were frequently at war, some churchmen were bloated on money and power and the abuse of both, the earliest Crusades were mounted, a mini-Renaissance flourished, and several spiritual movements appeared to call the Church back from its worldly ambitions to the message of Christ. In 1209, Francis received a vision in which Christ said, "Francis, Francis, go and repair my house which, as you can see, is falling into ruins." Later that year he was to write the Primitive Rule and his earliest companions joined him in the Order of Friars Minor, the Little Brothers. By the time Francis died in 1226, he had four thousand followers and by 1260 there were thirty thousand Franciscans. Something powerful had been unleashed by Francis and his early and important disciple, Clare of Assisi. Clare was the first woman to write a monastic rule for women, and her commitment to corporate poverty was as admirable as Francis'. Ever since, the world inside and outside the Church has been enticed and fascinated by it.

As nearly everyone knows, at the heart of Franciscan spirituality is the love of poverty, of simplicity, of living in peace, and of being in harmony with the created order. Is it any wonder this spirituality still speaks to us today? What is less well known, but central for Francis, is the constant call to being converted to the poor and crucified Christ, a deep communion with the Church, a life of prayer that is personal, communal, and liturgical, and a life lived in joy.

Anyone who wants to be a reformer has to take Franciscan spirituality seriously inside or outside the Church. Francis even loved the broken Church and unfair world of the twelfth century. He loved humanity so much that his way of reforming it was not to rant and rave (though later Franciscans became some of the best debaters in Europe), but to model and embody the very reform he sought. Francis is the patron saint of those who talk the talk *and* walk the walk. Even if his opponents were against what he was saying, they could not doubt his personal integrity. Most of his enemies are lost to history. Francis is a saint and the founder of a worldwide movement that nurtures prayer across the faith-spectrum to this day.

In recent years, of course, Francis and Clare have been reborn as patron saints of living with integrity with the environment, and rightly so. Francis articulated the ethic of the seamless garment of life long before the term was crafted. These days Franciscan spirituality reminds us that the issue of caring for the environment is a constitutive part of our Christian commitment to justice, for while the earth has been entrusted to us as stewards, to be preserved, it is also given into our hands to be developed in such a way that there will be a productive earth for future generations to inherit.

We can see how Francis' call to simplicity for all complements the contemporary call to limit our consumption, change our priorities in regard to energy and trade, and show the Third World the way to develop eco-friendly industries. Whatever our take might be on how we care for the created order, most of us know that we cannot keep going as we are, with ever-increasing unsustainable demands on our planet. Francis knew that the Old and New Testaments were filled with the importance of our relationships to the earth. In the Book of Genesis, humanity is told to care for and subdue the earth, not wreck it. Avarice is not one of the seven deadly sins for nothing.

Franciscan spirituality is not just about finding God in nature. It is that, and may it keep calling us to it. It is also that our stand for justice always takes into account the care our earth requires so that we have a productive planet to hand on to our children, and may we hand it on to them in better shape than we found it.

Franciscan spirituality is the gift that keeps giving.

CARMELITE SPIRITUALITY

When some people even hear the word *Carmelite* they think of silent nuns. Some others know a few of their most celebrated members like St. Teresa of Avila, St. John of the Cross, St. Thérèse of Lisieux, St. Teresa Benedicta of the Cross (Edith

Stein), among many others. While Carmelite spirituality is all of these, it is much more besides. The Carmelites have their roots in the twelfth-century movement of lay hermits in Europe who wanted to live like the desert fathers and mothers, in caves and in desperate poverty. Sometime after 1139, some of these hermits made the pilgrimage to Israel and joined other hermits who were living in caves around Mount Carmel. By 1206 they had elected a leader, had a primitive structure, and asked for a Way of Life to be approved. The Rule of St. Albert was established by 1214. A simple document, it said the Carmelite life was to be marked by solitude, continuous prayer, silence, fasting, perpetual abstinence from meat, manual work, vocal recitation of the psalms, the chapter of faults, and attendance at Mass.

By 1247, with a revised rule now approved by the pope, the Carmelites were established in Europe. They flourished, but the order moved from being rustic rural hermits to highly educated and begging priests living in urban monasteries. The first Carmelite nuns were admitted in 1452. Carmelite history is filled with minor and major reforms, calling for the re-establishment of the older, more primitive lifestyle. Two of the greatest reformers are also some of our most extraordinary mystics, St. Teresa of Avila and St. John of the Cross.

Carmelite spirituality centers on turning away from the world as a way to encounter the presence of God more fully. Following the example of Elijah, who had to pass through the desert in order to reach Mount Horeb, the mountain of God, this school teaches that one must master sinfulness (the desert) and be purified in God's love (contemplation) so that we might contemplate God's presence (the mountaintop). The way for this to happen for Carmelite monks, nuns, and laypeople is solitude, self-denial, and devotion to Our Lady. Their Marian devotion is based on seeing Mary as sister and mother and enabling us to keep saying yes to God in the same way she did. Since the fifteenth century, they have brilliantly integrated a stark lifestyle, the promotion of the affect, and sometimes mystical prayer, as well as a rigorous intellectual tradition. The Carmelite family also has a strong prophetic edge to their identity. When Elijah came down from the mountaintop, he had no trouble speaking the truth in love to those who needed to hear it. Carmelite saints and martyrs testify that there is no resurrection without embracing the cross. Carmelite spirituality embodies a countercultural, prophetic stance to this day.

While we can see the common elements with other spiritual families in the Church, the Carmelite emphasis on the importance of the desert of solitude even in the noise of a city stands out. And just when we might think that going into this solitude is running away, as some people say of enclosed orders of nuns, for example, it is clear these commentators have never done it. If you want to run away from your life, do not run to a contemplative order. There is nothing like solitude to bring us face-to-face with what our life is really like, for better or worse. To enable us to achieve this journey with emotional safety, Carmelite contemplation encourages us to engage in *kataphatic mysticism*, or the mysticism of light, where we encounter God in such a way that a suffusion of light illuminates our experience and knowledge. As St. Teresa of Avila says in *The Interior Castle*, "The brilliance of this inner vision is like that of an infused light coming from a sun covered by something as transparent as a properly cut diamond." This divine light allows us to illuminate the issue in our lives, our destiny, and our directions. This suffusion of light and joy has become a hallmark of religious experience.

St. John of the Cross, however, also knew what it was like to get stuck in the desert, where there was no light at all. *The Dark Night of the Soul* is not just the name of his most famous work; it has become a catchphrase in Western society to describe a period of serious difficulty. For John of the Cross, the dark night we enter into is *apophatic mysticism*, a conceptual darkness where we empty the mind as much as possible of what plagues us so that we may encounter the light of God's presence and through which we may receive a purification of memory. I have not met a sane spiritual person who went to the mountaintop and stayed there. The Carmelite tradition gives credibility and rigor to the valleys into which we all descend. It is not clinical depression; these times are when, because we have come closer to God, we become even more aware of the destructiveness in our lives and the things that immobilize us. In this experience, there is what John of the Cross calls a purification of memories. I don't know anyone who doesn't need the hard-won peace that comes through this.

DOMINICAN SPIRITUALITY

It is a very brave Jesuit who tries to confidently outline the Dominican school of spirituality. Not that it should be like that because our founder Ignatius Loyola was deeply inspired by St. Dominic. In fact, just as Ignatius was inspired by St. Benedict, St. Dominic, and St. Francis of Assisi, St. Dominic was equally inspired by St. Augustine. Or, more precisely, Dominican spirituality is based in the Rule of St. Augustine, a series of documents written about the year 400 as a guide to religious life. But if I am brave enough to provide a wholly inadequate pen-portrait of desert, Benedictine, Franciscan, and Carmelite spiritualities, then I can do my best with the great spiritual legacy of St. Dominic.

The Order of Preachers was officially recognized in 1216, but St. Dominic founded a community of religious women in 1206 and then a community of men in 1241. Because European bishops at the time were so busy administering their feudal estates, they were neglecting their office to preach and teach, especially outside the cities and major towns. Dominic and his companions saw a great need and filled it brilliantly. From the start, the Order of Preachers attracted articulate and intelligent men. At the heart of Dominican spirituality is contemplation on the truth in all its forms: in personal and communal prayer, and in studying, reading, teaching, and preaching. The motto of the order is simple and powerful: *Veritas* (Truth).

Though the Dominicans are friars, unlike the Benedictines they live in community as a base from which to go and preach. They were a product of emerging city culture of the high medieval period. Like their contemporaries the Franciscans, they were committed to poverty and so became famous as the "begging preachers," living off whatever donations they received. Unlike many preachers of the thirteenth century, they did not preach in Latin but in the vernacular language, so that their message would be immediate and effective. The Dominican way of life is characterized by *"Laudare, Benedicere, Praedicare"* ("to praise, to bless, and to preach"), and to do that effectively the community is ordered around prayer, study, community life, and ministry. One of the most extraordinary features of this spiritual school is that for almost all of its eight hundred years it has had laymen and laywomen as an integral part of the Dominican family. They too are called to seek the truth, pray, study, and preach in any way they can, mainly through the witness of their lives.

One of the elements Dominic stressed was to do penance for the sins of the world. Prayer, penance, and fasting are core elements of their lives and their preaching. Another famous feature of the earliest Dominicans was the way they developed and promoted the recitation of the Rosary. For illiterate people, this was a way of grounding their spirituality in the joyful, sorrowful, and glorious mysteries of the life of Jesus in the New Testament. It was genius to both invite people to prayer and to teach them the basic faith at the same time.

We can start to see there is nothing new about the New Age: beads, mantras, the search for the truth, and a life lived simply.

This school has been new for eight hundred years. So much of the Dominican school resonates with the contemporary spiritual search. The location of this movement in the cities is significant, where there is not just trade in commerce, but also a marketplace of ideas. In such a world of competing truths, the way to the truth is through contemplation, weighing up the arguments for or against truth in the light of faith *and* reason. Is it any wonder that this tradition has given the Church some of its finest thinkers?

The challenge, too, to live simply remains constant. As Dominic intuited, our lifestyle and our prayer are related. The most effective personal prayer is often the most pared-back and starkly simple, and the same goes for our day-to-day living. A right relationship with people and things enables vulnerability before life that reflects the vulnerability we take before God.

I am struck by the early insistence on preaching in the vernacular. As grand and sometimes beautiful as public liturgies can be, at its best any meditation on the Word, and the mediation of it, should be immediate and effective. Finding a way to speak God's Word to a world that cannot or will not hear is as challenging now as it was in the thirteenth century. It's in this context that prayers like the Rosary make sense. I want to say more about this in a future chapter but, for now, the way the Dominicans used a repetitious mantra prayer to bring people back to the basics of Jesus' life still inspires.

Sometimes that Word calls us to conversion, to repentance, and to reconciliation, which has never been an easy message to proclaim. It is just essential, lying as it does at the heart of the Gospel—turning away from anything that holds us back from loving God, loving our neighbor, and truly loving ourselves. As I said in *Where the Hell Is God,* I strongly believe prayer, penance, and fasting matter. Not because they change an unchanging God. They don't. We cannot get God to love us more. These ancient practices have stood the test of time in changing us, in breaking down resistances, and in being a response to God's invitation to a new and better life. With some types of prayer, all fasting, and every penance, we need to make sure the intention and the outcome come from a very healthy place within us for a wholly good purpose.

Finally, the fact that this spirituality has always had a lay expression says something of how multilayered it is. Other spiritual schools have lay members as well. The Franciscans, Benedictines, Norbertines, Carmelites, and Missionaries of Charity are a few of the biggest. There are thousands of Third Order Dominicans in the world today, formally vowed to the wider Dominican family. Any Third Order that has given us St. Catherine of Siena, St. Rose of Lima, St. Louis de Monfort, and Blessed Pier Giorgio Frassati has a lot going for it. Contemplative monasticism is a movable feast. It is an affair of the heart and an engagement of the mind as much as where my physical body may be. I can create a monastery where I am. It also keeps alive the critical missionary idea in the Gospel that preaching the good news is not reserved to clerics. It is the task and responsibility of all the followers of Christ. While a homily at a liturgy, by definition, can only be given by a deacon, priest, or bishop, a layperson may preach within a liturgy. Away from the liturgy, they must preach in any way they can, because they are baptized.

IGNATIAN SPIRITUALITY

If Dominican spirituality found an audience among laypeople, Ignatian spirituality was devised by a layman for laypeople, at least in its first expression. Iñigo Lopez de Loyola, later known as St. Ignatius of Loyola, was born in the Basque region of northern Spain in 1491. He was a person of many gifts: personal courage, great leadership, a strong and charming personality, honed diplomatic skills. While recuperating from a cannonball blast at the battle of Pamplona, he began reading a life of Christ and the lives of the saints and noted how he felt after this reading, in comparison to the feelings that followed from his daydreams about worldly success and conquests. It was the beginning of his carefully noting the movements of God's spirit in his life and his response to them. These thoughts of Iñigo were to become the basis of the *Spiritual Exercises*. Although he worked on the *Exercises* until he died in 1556, they were largely written in a cave at Manresa where he lived as a penitent and hermit in 1522. From there he studied at several universities, incurred the wrath of the Dominicans and the Spanish Inquisition, and gathered like-minded university students around him in Paris, who, in time, became the Jesuits. Later Ignatius was ordained a priest. He had such a love for Jesus that he wanted the group called the "Companions of Jesus," but some cardinals in the Vatican thought that comprised all the baptized, so in 1540 he was allowed to call his group the "Society" of Jesus.

IgnatianSpirituality.com has composed "Ten Elements of Ignatian Spirituality," which I have edited here for space:

1. It begins with a wounded soldier daydreaming on his sickbed.

    For Ignatius it all starts in personal experience. Who am I before God? A loved sinner.

2. "The world is charged with the grandeur of God."

    This line from a poem by the Jesuit Gerard Manley Hopkins captures a central theme of Ignatian spirituality: its insistence that God is at work everywhere—in work, relationships, culture, the arts, the intellectual life, creation itself. Ignatian spirituality places great emphasis on discerning God's presence in the everyday activities of ordinary life. It sees God as an active God, always at work, inviting us to an ever-deeper walk.

3. It's about call and response—like the music of a Gospel choir.

An Ignatian spiritual life focuses on God at work *now*. It fosters an active attentiveness to God joined with a prompt responsiveness to God. God calls; we respond.

4. "The heart has its reasons of which the mind knows nothing."

   This spirituality places great emphasis on the affective life: the use of imagination in prayer, discernment and interpretation of feelings, cultivation of great desires, and generous service.

5. Free at last.

   Ignatian spirituality emphasizes interior freedom. To choose rightly, we should strive to be free of personal preferences, superfluous attachments, and preformed opinions. Our one goal is the freedom to make a wholehearted choice to follow God.

6. "Sum up at night what thou hast done by day."

   The distinctive Ignatian prayer is the Daily Examen, a review of the day's activities with an eye toward detecting and responding to the presence of God. Three challenging, reflective questions lie at the heart of the *Spiritual Exercises*, the book Ignatius wrote, to help others deepen their spiritual lives: "What have I done for Christ? What am I doing for Christ? What ought I to do for Christ?"

7. A practical spirituality.

   Ignatian spirituality is adaptable. It is an outlook, not a program; a set of attitudes and insights, not rules or a scheme. At the heart of Ignatian spirituality is a profound humanism. It respects people's lived experience and it honors the vast diversity of God's work in the world.

8. Don't do it alone.

Ignatian spirituality places great value on collaboration and teamwork; on friendship and the need to have a spiritual director who helps interpret the spiritual movements.

9. "Contemplatives in action."

Those women and men—priests, religious, and laypeople—formed by Ignatian spirituality are often called "contemplatives in action." They unite themselves with God by joining God's active labor to save and heal the world.

10. "Men and women for others."

The early Jesuits often described their work as simply "helping souls." The great Jesuit leader Pedro Arrupe updated this idea and said it was about being "men and women for others." Both phrases express a deep commitment to social justice and a radical giving of oneself to others.

Ignatius did not found monasteries and did not want Jesuits to be monks. He wanted Jesuits to be "friends in the Lord." He founded no Ignatian Order for women, though some women's orders later followed his spirituality very closely. There was no Third Order or Lay Association, though lay Ignatian groups, especially the Christian Life Community, have flourished for the last hundred years. For Ignatius it was all about deepening an intimate relationship with Jesus that impels us to serve Christ in the world through the mission of the Church.

I may be the only Jesuit who will tell you this, but St. Ignatius was in fact an obsessive, compulsive, neurotic nut. That's not fair, of course, because he was also a genuinely holy, mystical and brilliant man of his time, but some of his behavior can easily lead us to conclude that my comment is neither facetious nor unwarranted. In fact, one of the most important chapters in his life gives the key to why Ignatian spirituality has been so enduring and adaptable. I want to take you back to the cave at Manresa in 1522. This was where Ignatius had his best and worst days. Unlike several of the other founders we have looked at, Ignatius dictated an autobiography and we know from it, and from letters he later wrote, that it was in that cave that his Rules for the Discernment of Spirits, arguably his greatest gift to the Church, were formed. That cave was also the scene of some very dangerous behavior.

We know that on the way to the Abbey of Montserrat (from where he left for Manresa) he encountered a Muslim man who defamed the Virgin Mary. Iñigo was so offended he wanted to kill him, but he could not decide whether to do it or not. Just ahead, there was a fork in the road, so he let the reins on his donkey go loose and if the donkey chose to go the same way as the Muslim, he decided he would murder him. If it took the other path, he would not. Thank God the donkey had more sense than Iñigo! In the cave, we know Ignatius-the-penitent whipped himself three times a day for months, wore an iron girdle, fasted on bread and water which he begged, slept very little and then on the ground, spent up to seven hours on his knees at prayer, covered his face with dirt, grew his hair and beard rough, and allowed his dirty nails to grow to a grotesque length. We also know that he suffered from spiritual scruples so badly he considered committing suicide by throwing himself into the River Cardonner. We would now diagnose the 1522 Ignatius as being an at-risk self-harmer, suffering from an acute depressive disorder and exhibiting suicidal behavior.

Thank God, two things saved him. First, because he was a soldier, he was used to taking orders from legitimate authorities and following them. When his Dominican Confessor at Manresa saw how far Ignatius was mentally and spiritually deteriorating, he ordered him, under holy obedience, to eat food, bathe, cut his hair and nails, stop the penances, and look after himself. Ignatius had to obey. From there on in Ignatius turned a corner and emerged a wise and holy man. Second, Manresa changed him forever—not just because he had undergone these terrible experiences and lived to tell the tale, but because he *reflected carefully* on how good things like prayer, penance, and fasting can quickly become instruments of self-destruction, in the name of God.

Ignatian spirituality works for those of us who may have glimpsed a dark place and found a way back from the abyss. Its wisdom in regard to the careful discernment of spirits was won in the face of staring down some very destructive demons indeed. No wonder people still find contemporary resonances in it.

Why bother praying? Because our tradition gives us a supermarket of ideas, styles, insights, challenges, and ways and means to God. If we want to belong to one school, we can. If we want to pick and choose what works for us at any stage of our life, then that's fine too. What we do know is that some of the people who became versed in these schools, along with the scores of other schools we have not explored, have led heroic lives of love in service of God and humanity. If "by their fruit you shall know them" is any recommendation, and it is, then these religious vineyards have, and still are, producing a rich harvest of flavors, textures, adaptability, hardiness, intensity, and abundant yields. They are worth tasting.

Chapter 5

It Comes Down to Jesus

It comes as no surprise that every model and every school of Christian prayer leads to Jesus Christ. As Christians we are the only world religion to believe that our God took our flesh and bone. The fine Scottish poet and musician and Church of Scotland clergyman, John Bell, writes of Advent:

> Light looked down and saw the darkness.
> "I will go there," said light.
> Peace looked down and saw war.
> "I will go there," said peace.
> Love looked down and saw hatred.
> "I will go there," said love.
> So he,
> the Lord of Light,
> the Prince of Peace,
> the King of Love,
> came down and crept in beside us.

"…[C]rept in beside us": what an insightful way to describe the way in which, without fanfare and in poverty, Jesus entered our time and place.

So Christian prayer should lead to Jesus. You might recall from the introduction to this book, that one of my correspondents told me, "God's answer to all prayers is Jesus Christ—end of story." At one level, I agree. God cannot do more for us than in the saving life, death, and resurrection of Jesus. However, the application of that to our daily life and struggles in prayer is quite a different thing. It reminds me of the story about the formidable Jesuit who was giving the first communicants instruction on how we receive the Bread of Life in the Eucharist. Trying to be a trendy catechist, he thought he would borrow from what he was teaching the children in science class—how animals collect food for their young. So he asked the class, "What's small and furry and eats nuts?" The class was in stunned silence. He tried again. "What's small and furry and eats nuts?" Still no response. So he picked on poor Tommy in the front row. "Tommy Ryan, you know the answer to this question like you know your own name. What's small and furry and eats nuts?" To which Tom looked up and sheepishly replied, "This is religion class, Father, and the answer to all your questions in religion class is 'Our Lord and Savior Jesus Christ,' but it sounds like a bloody squirrel to me." The answer is not always and everywhere and simply Jesus. Prayer to Christ is a little more complex than that.

JESUS CAN DEAL WITH COMPLEX HUMANITY

Let's start by looking at the least-read and least-prayed-over section of the Gospels. In fact, it is assigned as the Gospel for the Christmas Vigil Mass every year, but (wisely, I think) when confronted with a church full of families, most pastors go for the shepherd and angels from the Midnight Mass Gospel. It is, of course, the genealogy of Jesus. There are two versions: Matthew 1:1–17 and Luke 3:23–38.

Writing for a dominantly Jewish Christian audience, Matthew goes back to Abraham, the father of faith. Writing for a dominantly Gentile Christian audience, Luke goes back before the chosen people to Adam. As they progress, the names are almost identical between Abraham and David and then the two accounts vary considerably, coming together again in Joseph, who is not announced in either list as the father of Jesus but as the spouse of Mary, the mother of Jesus.

I want to focus on Matthew's genealogy. There are forty-two names in the list. He leaves out several significant Old Testament people that should be there, such as Ahaziah, Joash, Jotham, and Jehoakim. It would appear Matthew wanted forty-two generations from David to Jesus, because of the symmetry of multiples of seven, the perfect number. Why does any of this matter to our prayer?

The power of the genealogy of Jesus is lost on us today, but it would not have been lost on its first audience. In Matthew's list, we find heroic models of faith and self-sacrifice: Abraham, Isaac, Judah, Nashon, Jehoshaphat, Uzziah, Jotham, Hezekiah, Josiah, Zerubbabel, Joseph, and Mary. There are several names of people whose names are mentioned in the Old Testament, but that is about it. We assume they were honorable men: Perez, Hezron, Ram, Amminada, Salmon, Boaz, Obed, Jesse, Joram, Shealtiel, and Abiud. And then things get interesting. Jeconiah was king during Judah's worst chapter when they were deported to Babylon as slaves. Jacob started out badly but became good. David and his son Solomon start out well enough but end up very mixed blessings for Israel. Urriah, Abijah, and Asa were punished for displeasing the Lord. Rehoboam, Ahaz, Manasseh, and Amon were ruthless, murderous tyrants. Talk about doing genealogy, as on the Australian television program *Find My Family*; I am not sure anyone would want to find these men in the family tree. We have eight men we have never heard of, or at least they are not recorded in any of the books of the Old Testament: Eliakim, Azor, Zadok (not the famous one), Achim, Eliud, Eleazar, Matthan, and Jacob (not the famous one). Maybe they were in the oral history of the time, but they are lost to us now. And then it gets better still: the women.

Only five women are mentioned by Matthew. Each conceived a child in what could only be described as complex circumstances: Tamar, the wronged widow of Genesis, gets her own back by seducing her father-in-law and was vindicated for her courage. Rahab was a Canaanite woman in prostitution who bravely aided the Hebrews to enter the Promised Land by spying for them. Ruth starts out life as a Moabite. They were despised by the Jews. She converts to Judaism but is a poor, childless widow until she meets Boaz and ends up being the great-grandmother of King David. Bathsheba is not mentioned by name, but commits adultery with King David, becomes pregnant, and then David has her husband killed to cover up his sin. Marrying David, her abuser, she becomes the mother of Solomon. Finally, there is Mary who conceives by the power of God. So these five women all become mothers in extremely unusual circumstances.

I love the genealogy of Jesus because at the very start of the Gospel it places human beings in all their complexity at the center of the drama. It shows that good can eventually triumph despite the most evil of actions; that good comes even if your story is lost to us now; and that even in events that first appear to be a disaster, a revelation can emerge.

IF WE ARE PRAYING TO JESUS, OUR RELATIONSHIPS ARE TRANSFORMED

Matthew tells us that relationships matter. That's what the Trinity is all about. We do not speak, preach, or teach much about the Trinity these days. I think that's a mistake. I think it's because we can get caught into trying to work out a mathematical impossibility: three into one. I know when I was a child I was not given many stimulating images of the Trinity. There was the old man in the sky, the son on the cross, and the bird! Others have given us helpful images in regard to the Trinity. St. John of Damascus said the Trinity was a dance, a *pas de trois*. St. Ignatius Loyola described it as three notes in a single chord. St. Patrick famously used the three-leaf clover as a teaching aid to get the point across to the Irish, and St. Augustine thought the Trinity acted in unison in the same way that memory, intelligence, and will does within each of us.

Some people in their prayer, however, find it easier to address God the Father (or Mother), or others are more focused on the Holy Spirit. In our theology of the Trinity, we hold that the Trinity is co-equal, co-eternal, and co-substantial. In other words, the Father and the Spirit never get jealous if the Son gets more attention than they do. And the Son and Father are fine with charismatics who give the Holy Spirit the credit for everything. The persons within the Trinity empower each other, and are equally present in every act of God in the world, be it in creating, redeeming, or making holy. But at some stage, our prayer is made "through Christ our Lord Amen."

It took the early Christians four hundred years to grasp fully what Jesus was about when he spoke of his relationship to the Father and Spirit. They struggled to understand how and why God would have three faces and yet exist as One, love as One, act as One. They knew the core of God was not an idea or a principle, but was a loving relationship. Furthermore, the early Christians knew that all of humanity was invited into this relationship.

Think about this for a minute: we pray because we believe that the God who creates, redeems, and sustains the world seeks us out and invites us into a loving relationship.

Not that we can pretend that relationships are easy. I like the story of the time when Satan makes an appearance at the front of the Church during Mass. Everyone realizes immediately who it is and runs away as fast as they can, yelling and screaming. Everyone except for Mrs. Smith. She stayed put. Satan goes up to her and says, "Don't you realize who I am?" "Oh, I know who you are alright—you're Satan, you're the devil incarnate." "Aren't you frightened of me? Everyone else seemed to be frightened of me." "Not me," said Mrs. Smith nonchalantly. "Why not?" Satan retorted. "Because, listen here, Satan, I have been married to your brother for the last sixty-one years!"

I said earlier that as Christians we have personal faith, not private faith. The quality of our relationships reflects to the world the quality of our prayer. It's not what we say that people will remember as much as who we are and what we do. For example, when I think about my school days, I can only remember about ten actual classes over the twelve years, and then for varying reasons. My teachers did their job. I was well set-up for further and higher studies. It's just that I don't recall many of the details of the lessons. What I can recall, however, is my relationship with every teacher I ever had, for better or worse. I was taught by women and men who loved their profession and went above and beyond the call of duty in educating us. I was also taught by people who did not like kids! Not that they ever said that directly. It was just that they screamed it at us loudly and clearly everyday by their actions and attitudes. I have no idea what they were doing in a classroom. Not that a teacher always has to like an adolescent. There is plenty not to like, but most of us would expect that you should not teach in a school if you resent or dislike children.

If ever I needed a role model for how Christian prayer forms and informs relationships I just think of my first grade teacher, Sister Mary Consuelo. Behind her back, we called her Sister-Mary-consume-a-whalelo. She was a Sister of Mercy. She was firm and fair. She needed to be. She once told me that in the forty-four years of her teaching career, she never had less than forty children in class. She once had sixty-one children in the same room. There were forty-two children in my first grade class in 1969. Could you imagine that ratio now? I also thought Sister was tall. She was five foot one. In second grade, Sister also prepared us for our first confession, as it was then called, and our first Holy Communion. I remember being so terrified going into the dark box to make my first confession, that when the slide pulled back, I could barely see through the grill so in my anxiety I started yelling on top note, "Bless me, Father, for I have sinned, this is my first confession, and these are my sins." At that point the Dean of the Cathedral said, "God's not deaf and neither am I!"

I wish I could say that I had really looked forward to my first Holy Communion because I wanted to receive the Lord in a special and unique way. But that would be a lie. Actually, I was terrified of doing something wrong at the Mass and of biting the host. At the age of seven, what I was really looking forward to was the party that followed the Mass and the presents I would get. When back at school the day after my Communion, Sr. Mary Consuelo asked me what gift I enjoyed the most. Of all the Bibles, holy pictures, rosaries, and medals I received, the gift I treasured was a bone china holy water font of the madonna and child. "I would like to see that," Sr. Mary Consuelo said. "Would you bring it to school tomorrow?"

The next day, during the first break, little lunch we used to call it, Sister was on playground duty. She was wearing a large blue and white striped apron over her habit. Imagine this scene. There were over seven hundred children in my Catholic primary school, and there was only one teacher supervising all of us. 1:700. That be would illegal today. Not that Sister-Mary-consume-a-whalelo had any trouble controlling the masses. She was a formidable figure who was as wide as she was tall, and ruled the playground with a whistle. Do you remember how big the nun's pockets were in those habits? Seemingly, the nuns carried everything in there and they could put their hands on what they needed at a moment's notice. I raced up to Sister who was surrounded by children. "I've brought the holy water font, Sister." "Very good, go and get it." I carefully took the font, all wrapped up in tissue paper, out of my bag and then ran down to the asphalt playground. I was so excited at showing off my favorite present that right in front of Sister I tripped and down I went. The font hit the asphalt too. It did not just break. No, it smashed, and into tiny pieces. Sister swung into action. She was an old hand at health and safety, long before the term was invented. Into her pocket she went. Out came the whistle and with a full, shrill blast seven hundred children froze in their places. Sister said to the children in our vicinity, "Whoever picks up the most pieces of china will get a holy picture." We thought that was something back then.

The second whistle rang out, and while six hundred fifty children resumed their games, fifty children did a forensic search of the area picking up every piece visible to the naked eye and dropping them in the hammock Sister had made from her apron with her left arm. Meanwhile I was so distraught that Consuelo's right arm brought me in for a very big hug. Sister had many gifts, but among them God had also given her a very ample bosom. In fact, whenever we read about God's deep and consoling breasts in Isaiah 66:11, I go back to the second grade.

The bell went and Sister rolled up the apron and walked me back to class. Three weeks later, she told me to stay in during recess. I thought I was in trouble. When every other child had left the room, she opened the drawer of her desk and there wrapped up in new tissue paper was a fully restored holy water font. By then I think I had forgotten about it.

In those days, we knew nothing much about the Sisters. They went to Mass, said their prayers, and taught school. Before Sister Mary Consuelo became a nun, however, she had done a degree in art, majoring in watercolors and ceramics. She had taken those hundreds of fragments and spent hours and hours piecing back together my holy water font. When it was set, she repainted the entire object. The only sign that it had ever been broken was the rough plaster of Paris on the back. She could have thrown those pieces away and I would have gotten over it. In fact, I had. But such was the effect of her prayer life on her relationships, even with a seven-year-old boy, that she spent what must have been most of her leisure time for weeks reconstructing a treasured gift. But she was the real gift that day, and it the best lesson I had from her.

I am not an overly sentimental person when it comes to things, and I have been privileged to have studied or worked in Australia, the United Kingdom, Italy, and the United States. But everywhere I go to live, that font goes too. Soon after I was ordained a priest in December of 1993, I was honored to be asked to preside at the Eucharist at Emmaus, the Sisters of Mercy nursing home at Brisbane. Sitting in her usual spot in the front row was Sister Mary Consuelo, now aged eighty-four. As part of my homily, I told the other hundred sisters the story of the holy water font. When I was done and sat down, Sister got up from her place and turned around to the others and said, "I told you I was good!" She was very good indeed. At that time, she knew she was dying. She talked about it openly and calmly. She was so serene. "I'm looking forward to going home and meeting Christ face-to-face," she said gently as we said our goodbyes. It was the last time I saw her, a frail wizened figure waving goodbye. As I drove away, I said to myself, "If that sense of peace and dignity in the face of death is what a lifetime of prayer gives you, bring it on."

SEEING THE FACE OF CHRIST

Sister's comment that she was longing to see the face of Christ sums up what the point of Christian faith is all about. For centuries, if Catholics were asked why they prayed, went to the sacraments, or did charitable works, they would have answered, "to save my soul" or "to get to Heaven." This is true, and Jesus certainly links our life in this world with our destiny in the next, but we need to be careful of two extremes. First, we cannot earn or buy salvation. It is God's free gift of saving grace. We respond to this grace by good works and the way we live and pray. As strong as Jesus is in some parts of the Gospel talking about sheep and goats and final judgment, there are even more passages where the portrait of the Father he presents is ridiculously compassionate and completely merciful. And because Jesus is the face of God for the world, we know that he never inflicted pain on people, that he was the embodiment of God's forgiveness, and that he went out of his way to reach out to those who were despised and rejected in his own society. We live in the tension between God's total love of us and God's justice where he will call us to account for the very serious things we have freely and knowingly done or failed to do. Second, the emphasis on saving my soul can overstate an individualistic spirituality with an attitude that goes: "I can't save anyone else, so all I can do is put my head down and save my own soul." It is true that only God saves, but Jesus also told us that, for his followers, the reign of God is something that should also be here and now. Working, and sometimes fighting, for a more just world must be a constitutive part of our life and our prayer. It is not an either/or. It is a both/and.

In a previous chapter, we looked at different names for God and how they influence the way we pray and what we believe. How we see Christ makes that insight even more particular. Sister Mary Consuelo wanted to meet Christ face to face, and that for her was not a frightening event at all. Her image of Christ was warm and tender. So how we picture Christ really matters. As a more creative way into this idea, let's think about how, for better and sometimes for worse, the film industry has shaped the values, questions, sensibilities, and images in regard to almost everything in Western society. This includes, whether we like it or not, religious images as well. Since the advent of the cinema, there have been at least twenty-two major portrayals of Jesus on the silver screen.

The Salvation Army made *Soldiers of the Cross* in 1901. In 1909, they made *Heroes of the Cross*. Tragically, in 1913, some anti-movie Salvationists denounced the cinema as an agent of the devil, the film units of the worldwide Salvation Army were closed down, and all films were ordered to be destroyed. Only fragments of these first two films have survived. The famous Pathé Company of France made several films of Christ's life from 1905–1910. These were the most popular films of their day. Sid Oldcock directed *From the Manger to the Cross* in 1912, and the great American director D. W. Griffiths shot various New Testament scenes in *Intolerance* of 1916. Cecil B. de Mille knew an epic story when he read one, and so he made *Kings of Kings* in 1927. By 1932, in the first film censorship legislation in the world, British censors decreed that there was should be "no nudity and no depiction of Jesus Christ" on the screen, so he had to become an off-camera extra in *Barabbas* of 1935. The French had no such problem and so Jesus is center stage in *Golgotha* in the same year.

The embargo on the Jesus story was still in place in the 1950s, but he makes background appearances in Henry Koster's *The Robe* of 1953, William Wyler's *Ben Hur* of 1959, and Frank Borbage's *The Big Fisherman* of 1959. It was not until Nicholas Ray's remake of *King of Kings* of 1961 that the Jesus story hit the big screen again in its own right. In 1965, Hollywood made the most expensive film then ever made with George Stevens' *The Greatest Story Ever Told*. It bombed at the box office and so the days of the Jesus epic were over. This film was littered with Hollywood's biggest stars of the time, but the best scene is where John Wayne as the Centurion at the foot of the cross drawls his one and only line in the film, "Truly, this man was the son of Gaad." It is claimed the director George Stevens had to do many takes of this scene and at one stage asked the Duke to emote more "with a sense of awe." During the next take, Wayne drawled with greater emphasis, "Aw, truly this man was the son of Gaad."

An Italian Marxist, Pier Palo Pasolini, made one of the more important Jesus films in 1964, *The Gospel According to Matthew*. That opened the floodgates for filmmakers to think very differently about the Gospel story. *Godspell* appeared in 1973 and for the first time ever Jesus was presented as a contemporary who sang and danced his way through his life and death and resurrection. *Jesus Christ Superstar* was released in the same year. Franco Zeffirelli's marathon *Jesus of Nazareth* came along in 1976, Dennis Potter's *Son of Man* in 1978, and Peter Sykes' *Jesus* in 1979.

Among the most controversial films set in the time of Jesus has him as a supporting character. Terry Jones' *Life of Brian* was released in 1979. I can remember when this film was released. Our pastor said, "It would be an occasion of mortal sin for any Catholic to see this film." Every sixteen-year-old in the parish went that afternoon. Equally controversial, but for very different reasons, was Martin Scorsese's *The Last Temptation of Christ* in 1988. And just when people might have been scared off the Jesus genre, the French Canadian, Denys Arcand, had a smash box office and critical hit with *Jesus of Montreal* in 1989.

Interestingly the 1990s did not see one major film about Jesus on the big screen. He moved to the small screen and especially to video. Then in 2003 Mel Gibson's *The Passion of the Christ* generated incomparable publicity and debate which has seen that film in the top hundred of the highest grossing films of all time, taking in $611 million worldwide.

Many of us have seen several of these films. Some of the images from them inform our prayer, and some of those are more helpful than others. But there are problems. Jesus on film is almost always handsome and white. Against all historical probability, Jesus sometimes has bright blue eyes. Except for Pasolini and Gibson, his Jewish faith has never been center stage, though his Judaism is front and center in three of the four Gospels. Yet can we pray to a Jesus who was black, or at least very dark brown, and who was a Jewish rabbi? Prayer is political when it challenges any latent racism or anti-Semitism in us.

Jesus has gone from being the image of a talking holy picture at the turn of the century, to being a matinee idol of heavenly significance; from being a hero who never gets the girl and never has a fist fight, to Pasolini's angry hero; from being a hippie leading flower-power love songs, to Brian's straight man in *The Life of Brian*. More recently, the story of Jesus' passion and death in *Jesus of Montreal* became an everyman tale, while Mel Gibson's graphic and savage portrait of Jesus' suffering and death was meant to shock, and it did.

We are still waiting for a filmmaker who takes each of the Gospel texts seriously enough not to conflate them into one story, allowing each of the inspired portraits of Jesus in Matthew, Mark, Luke, and John to be seen in their respective richness and detail. It would be good, one day, to have a Jesus film that also shows the context in which the story of Jesus was written, and the way we believe the Holy Spirit works in and through their experience in forming the text, and our experience in hearing it and living it out.

We might have to pray for a fresh and modern quartet of Jesus films entitled: "Mark," "Matthew," "Luke," and "John." If they did it to *The Lord of the Rings* and *Harry Potter*, I think we have a four-film series on Jesus ready to go.

IMPLICATIONS OF JESUS' FACE FOR OUR PRAYER

The Church has always known that iconography matters; that's why it has been so *proprietorial* about the images it allows and promotes. These days it can no longer control the image of

Christ and so his story and his saving role now compete with Superman, Batman, Ironman, and the Avengers. It has an impact on an increasingly unchurched society, who thinks that Jesus is just another incredible superhero. Christians, however, are not saved by a superhero; we are invited to enjoy the saving love of God in an ongoing relationship with the Father, the Son, and the Holy Spirit. For us Jesus is not the best of a good bunch. He is the definitive revelation of God for the world. And he was not a fictional character. He was born, he lived, he was put to death, and in faith we believe he was raised by God. Tacitus, Pliny, and Josephus all write about him, quite independently of the evidence of the New Testament.

And his life and ministry were not part of a good show. While one of Jesus' earliest titles was as a wonder-worker in the New Testament, "sign faith" is the weakest of all faith: "how blessed are those who have not seen but believe." Signs draw attention to themselves, and people end up believing in "the power," but Jesus wanted people who saw the signs to see the love of God and believe in God.

One of the reasons we pray to Jesus is that while Jesus saves us from the forces of evil and destruction, we are not passive in our salvation. While amazing grace is unearned and undeserved, it is not forced upon us. We can reject the invitation to faith. We pray that we keep accepting it and living it.

That said, it is also true that when we start to read and pray over the Gospels we can see that the radical edge of Jesus' life has been domesticated by the Church's tradition. He was by any reckoning a sane revolutionary. If we are never challenged and unsettled by Jesus' words in our all-too blessed lifestyles, we have to think about whose face we are seeing in our prayer. I like the old line that Jesus came "to afflict the comfortable and comfort the afflicted." At times, in our prayer, Jesus does both.

THE LORD'S PRAYER

If we want to be both challenged and confronted by Jesus in our prayer, we cannot go past the prayer he taught us.

One of the wonderful ironies in the present Catholic liturgy is that for all our attention to being exact in regard to the translation of the Latin into English, when it comes to the Lord's Prayer we still use the Anglican Archbishop Thomas Cranmer's 1539 translation of the Lord's Prayer. It is wonderful poetry, but it is not the most exact of translations. The eminent biblical scholar Joseph A. Fitzmyer, SJ, in *The Gospel According to Luke* looks at both Matthew and Luke's different versions of the Lord's Prayer and offers this middle way from the texts:

> Father Holy is your name
> Your kingdom come
> Give us today
> Our daily bread/food
> Forgive us our debts
> As we forgive our debtors
> and do not lead us to the test.

What a brief and elegant prayer! I think its brevity and simplicity only adds to its dignity. Sometimes we can think that we have to say long prayers to be heard and be serious. In Matthew, just two verses before Jesus teaches his famous prayer, he instructs the disciples not to "babble as the pagans do" because God already knows what is in our hearts as we start to pray. Less is almost always more. For example, did you know that Lincoln's Gettysburg address was 250 words long? The man before Lincoln spoke for over an hour. The man who followed Lincoln spoke for even longer. Today, no one remembers what they said. Lincoln's two and a half minutes, by contrast, changed United States history and the mentality of the Western world. Matthew's longer version of the Lord's Prayer—which, depending on the translation, has anywhere from thirty to fifty-six words—is another example of how a few sentences have changed history.

We declare that we belong to God in the most intimate of ways, as members of God's family, and therefore we belong to each other. We pray that God's kingdom will come here and how (through our gratitude for God's generosity and forgiveness), and we pray to be saved from being asked to be martyrs: the time of trial.

It is so easy to allow our faith lives to become compartmentalized. The Lord's Prayer breaks that wide open. For some, religious belief and practice fit into a nice little box that has no discernible influence on the rest of their lives. The old line goes, "Be careful what you pray because you might just get what you ask for." This prayer is the only one of which I am aware that unites the entire Christian family, and if all 2.1 billion of us lived these forty-two words, we would, in Christ's name, change the world.

Why bother praying? Because Christian prayer is not about appeasing an angry God. It is centered on a person, Jesus, and through him we are invited into a loving and saving relationship with the Father, Son, and Spirit that has consequences for how we live in this world and the next. In this relationship, nothing is wasted in our often-complex lives. We are invited where we are, as we are, to grow and become even more. And when we feel distant from Jesus, guess who has moved away from whom? There is nothing that can ever, or will ever, stop God from loving us. It is never too late to make a return.

Chapter 6

Public Prayer

Except under extraordinary circumstances, Christians not only have public faith but they also gather with other Christians to pray, especially on the Lord's Day.

In *Where the Hell Is God?* I only touched on the importance of liturgy to our prayer. I said there that "liturgies in all their styles and forms are not about the power of a larger number calling on a changeable God to roll over on a particular point. That would be a political rally. No, liturgy is where we join our personal prayer with the prayer of the assembled Church, the whole people of God, asking God to change us so that we might more reflect his loving face and thereby transform the world."

Indeed, in *The Catechism of the Catholic Church,* nos. 1068 and 1136–1140, the Church says that liturgy is primarily an action of Christ who gathers the whole community of the baptized to enter into full, conscious, and active participation in celebrations so that the faithful might go out and bear witness to Christ in the world. This is a pastoral issue today. There is now an increasing number of unchurched people who approach the Church to celebrate a baptism, wedding, or funeral. This is a good thing. They should be welcomed, supported, and encouraged. But it can be hard going because while the parents primarily want to announce their newborn to the world, the husband and wife want to celebrate their love for each other, or the family wants to celebrate the life of the one they mourn, the Church is focused on celebrating Christ. It is Christ who initiates and saves all the baptized. It is Christ whose sacrificial love for us finds a deep expression in married love. It is the mercy and love of Christ who receives our dead. You can start to see the pastoral tension. While it should never be an either/or, we have all been to some sacraments where Christ was lucky to get a mention amidst the celebration of the individuals involved. Take eulogies. The longest one I have ever sat through went for one hour and six minutes. And they say priests are long-winded! I knew we were in trouble when after forty minutes the eulogist said, "Then in 1963...." We still had a way to go. The tension in liturgy today is holding together that this celebration is not about an abstraction, it is Christ present and active in the lives of real people in real time. Both matter.

GOD COMES TO US IN OUR NEED

I learned more about why we pray in public liturgy during one of the most important liturgies of my life. I was ordained a priest at the Jesuit parish of North Sydney on December 11, 1993. I was ordained with a good friend, Michael McGirr. I was supposed to be ordained at Brisbane, the capital of my home state, but for a whole variety of Jesuit reasons I was asked to join Michael in Sydney. Despite being friends, I can remember being very anxious as I rang him with this suggestion, imagining he may prefer to be ordained on his own, in his home parish, where his family had been pillars of the parish for generations. After a pause in the conversation, which I mistakenly took to be displeasure, he said, "Well, Dickie" (Michael is one of the few people who get away with calling me that), "this is a huge relief. You're more interested in liturgy than I am, so why don't we agree that you organize the ceremony and I'll just turn up." It didn't quite work out like that, but it did move in that direction.

Christopher Willcock, SJ, our famous Australian Jesuit

composer, and I called in a few musician friends to help out. We put together a seventy-voice choir, the brass and timpani out of the Sydney Symphony Orchestra, and soloists from Opera Australia. As you can tell, it was a very simple, low-key event!

In planning that ordination, I missed two things. The first was that that summer's night would be one of the hottest and most humid days anyone could remember. The temperature got to 102 degrees (38 Celsius). When the ceremony started at eight p.m., it was still 82 degrees (27 Celsius). The second thing I missed in the planning was that on that night, directly across the road from the church on the North Sydney Oval, the Salvation Army was conducting "Carols by Candlelight." It started at eight p.m. as well. As the procession snaked its way to the back of the church and up the stairs, all we could hear from the loud speakers booming across the road was "I'm Dreaming of a White Christmas." I was so hot, that I was too!

Michael and I had eight hundred of our closest family and friends packed into this church with no air-conditioning. The competition from the Salvation Army, however, meant that the people at the back couldn't hear very well. Rather than anything of the ceremony, all they could hear was "Jingle Bells, Jingle Bells, Jingle All the Way." So what did they do? They closed the windows and doors. Watching this happen from the sanctuary was one thing, but then we felt a wave of heat roll up the church. More than a little nervous and under the lights and the vestments, I felt that the sanctuary had become a sauna.

During the singing of Fr. Willcock's splendid *Trocaire Gloria* I thought to myself, "I'm not feeling very well," and sat down. Then I thought, "I'm *really* not feeling very well," and went to put my head between my legs—which was not the pose I wanted to strike at my ordination. And as I did, I passed out on the floor.

Now, videos are wonderful things! Mine shows that as I sat down, my mother got out of the front pew, walked up on the sanctuary, and was there in time to catch me as I fell. I fell into my mother's arms. I have always thought that Sigmund Freud would have had a field day with this moment—widowed mother catches celibate priest son at his ordination: Oedipus, eat your heart out! My mother loves that part of the video, because not only does it capture her doing what she calls her "Pieta trick," but, because, as she explains, "That was the most expensive dress I have ever purchased in my life, and look, it fell beautifully on the floor. That dress was worth every cent I paid for it!"

I discovered that night that nothing stops a Father Christopher Willcock *Gloria*. When I asked him later what he would've done if I had died, he laughed and said, "I would have said, 'Ladies and gentlemen of the choir and the band, please turn to the *Requiem Mass* at the back.'"

Once the *Gloria* had concluded, the bishop—who was, for good measure, presiding at his first ordination ever—asked was there a doctor in the congregation. This was a Jesuit ordination, so soon I was surrounded by a team of twelve medicos and a couple of nurses. I could have had every part of my anatomy dealt with by a specialist. It was just a heavy faint, but when I came to, the bishop wondered aloud what to do next. My then-provincial, Fr. William Uren, SJ, told the bishop, "Well, we're not coming back tomorrow." And with that, Michael was dispatched to take me to the sacristy to have a walk around and a drink and to return when I was ready. When we got to the sacristy, I plaintively said to Michael, "I'm so sorry, Mick, I've ruined our ordination." "Don't be sorry, Dickie," he replied, "I'm not nervous at all now because I can't do anything more to muck this liturgy up than what you've already done."

Meanwhile, what was happening in the Church was a study in human nature. Because my father died of a stroke at the age of thirty-six, I knew my immediate and extended family would be anxious that a serious episode had occurred. On the other side of the aisle the McGirrs were understandably saying, "That Richard Leonard is such a show-off! It was our Michael's night too, and now the focus is all on him." Across the aisle, my side was filling in the McGirr side about our family's medical history. So much so that when Michael and I emerged from the sacristy, you would swear Lazarus had just come out of the tomb. After the mandatory canonical questions were asked and before we proceeded on, I knew that for my family's sake it was important that I speak so that they could be relieved that I had not suffered a stroke. The bishop agreed. I told the congregation, "You've just seen a perfectly planned liturgy go completely down the gurgler. So we better just get on with it." And the crowd burst into supportive applause all over again.

Later that night, a Jesuit theologian told me, "This was the best ordination I have ever attended." I was curious given that the style of music and liturgy that night would not have been to his taste. He tends to be a Kumbaya-My-Lord-on-a-bad-guitar kinda guy. "I don't know if you noticed," I replied, "but I passed out during the *Gloria*." "Yes, that's what made it really great." "How's that?" "Well," he went on excitedly, "as we were coming in the procession singing Chris' glorious arrangement of 'All Creatures of Our God and King,' you could not help but be filled with how great God is. And then within a short time you collapsed on the floor. It acted out the central drama of every liturgy: that God is great and we are frail. That God looks on us in our frailty and sent Christ to sustain and support us in and through the Church. We come to public prayer because in our frailty we need God's grace to help us witness to the Gospel. That's what made this the best ordination I have ever attended."

Why do we bother praying in public or private? Because God is great and we are frail and we need Christ's grace in and through the Church to help us witness to the Gospel.

SEVEN SPECIAL HELPS

The seven sacraments are unique moments where we believe God comes to us in special ways. Baptism, Eucharist, penance, confirmation, marriage, holy orders, and the anointing of the sick are, as St. Augustine says, "an outward and visible sign of an inward and invisible grace." There were only six sacraments for centuries. Do you know which one was the last one included? Although marriage was esteemed since the earliest days of the Church, it did not formally and finally enter the number of sacraments until Innocent IV, in the profession of faith prescribed for the Waldensians on the December 18, 1208, included marriage. There are wonderfully complex reasons why it took so long to formally include marriage, but preeminent among them is that sexual intercourse is a constitutive part of the sacrament and some theologians had difficulties with this. In fact, these days I think this is a stunning statement. We now teach that there is one sacrament where, unless you give your body in love to your husband or wife after you take your vows, then it is a null and void Christian marriage. No consummation, no sacrament.

The other reason some medieval theologians wanted to formally include marriage was because they wanted seven official sacraments rather than six. When we are praying over the scriptures and we come upon a number, it is good to recall that numbers are almost always symbolic in the Bible. One, three, seven, twelve, forty, and fifty have specific meanings. One is the number of unity, of God. Three is action of the Lord, the third day. There are in fact six active days of creation, two multiples of three, and on the seventh day, God has a rest—the oldest labor law in the world. Seven is the perfect number:

> And on the seventh day God finished the work that he had done, and he rested on the seventh day from all the work that he had done. So God blessed the

seventh day and hallowed it, because on it God rested from all the work that he had done in creation.

Twelve always represents the twelve tribes or the fulfillment of Israel. There are twelve patriarchs, twelve judges, twelve apostles, and Jesus is twelve when in Luke's Gospel he undertakes his first public ministry. Forty is the time of formation and is also found among many other examples: forty days of rain in Noah's flood, Moses' fast, Jesus in the desert, and the time between the resurrection and the ascension in Luke/Acts. And it was for forty years that the Israelites wandered in the desert. Fifty is the year of jubilee, usually celebrated only once in a person's lifetime where, among other things, the Israelites would set the slaves free, the fields were allowed to go fallow for a year, and all debts were forgiven. In Luke/Acts it is fifty days from Easter Day to Pentecost.

Of all the sacraments, the most important is baptism. Our Catholic instinct is say Eucharist, but there is no Eucharist without baptism. We can confidently say baptism may be the most important, but Eucharist is for many of us the most special. The other thing to pray on is that baptism is also the most ecumenical sacrament we have. It always has been, even in the terrible days of religious and sectarian bigotry. If an Anglican wants to become a Catholic, a Lutheran, a Presbyterian, a Methodist, an Orthodox, or an Episcopalian, he or she is never re-baptized. It is one Christ, one faith, one baptism. The only groups who re-baptize as a matter of course are the Baptists, who do not recognize infant baptism, and several of the evangelical churches because a full immersion baptism is the only one that is valid for them. It is true that the Greek word *bapto*, or *baptizo*, means to "to wash" or "to immerse," and so I think full immersion better represents what it intends, namely, Jesus' tomb. Because of the three days Jesus spent in the tomb, we plunge our adults and children into the watery tomb of the font three times. And as we do, we call on the Trinity to enable them to die to sin, and rise to the freedom of new life in Christ. In this context, we can see that the deeper the font and the fuller the immersion, the more easily everyone present understands the power of the symbols. That said, it is strange to me that groups who want to be so biblically literal about the amount of water used at baptism are not literal about the place of the water: the River Jordan. So volume matters, geography does not.

When we come to pray publicly, what links the sacraments? Apart from what was said earlier, they all require the Word of God to be read. They all have a rhythm and flow, action/contemplation. They all involve touch and engage the senses and they all mark a rite of passage.

THE WORD OF GOD LIVING NOW

I think Dan Brown did Christianity a favor in writing *The Da Vinci Code*. While its theories could be easily and humorously disproved, that novel, and that's all it was, started people doing something I have never witnessed before—talking about the origins and history of Christianity and the formation of the Bible at bars, parties, and over dinner. I spent five years of my life going to barbecues where, within the first ten minutes, someone would say, "Father, what did you think of *The Da Vinci Code*?" Fascinating conversations would ensue about topics of which adult Christians and Catholics had very little knowledge.

What this book, and later the film, did was to expose the level of ignorance among Christians about their own history and how the New Testament was compiled. It is much to our shame that Mr. Brown has been the first person to tell a host of biblically illiterate Catholics, and other Christians besides, that the New Testament was not a first-century version of the Book of Mormon falling from the sky. It's not Dan Brown's fault that the religious education of most of us was so poor that we were never told that the revelation of our sacred texts came through a prolonged, passionate fight over the centuries about what was in, and what was out. Hebrews, James, Revelation, and 1 and 2 Peter, and not the four canonical Gospels, were the highly disputed texts. It was not until 633 that, finally, the Council of Toledo decreed that the fights were over and that the twenty-seven books we now accept as the New Testament were it.

And it is not even the fault of most Catholics that we didn't know this, because we were warned off reading the Bible, and that the study of its history or compilation was a Protestant concern at best, or a sin against accepting it as Holy Writ. One of the best gifts of the Second Vatican Council has to be the promotion of the sacred scriptures for private prayer and study.

Given that *some prayer is better than no prayer* is one of the dictums of my life, wherever possible it should include some sort of meditation on the Word of God, especially the Gospel. These days there are all sorts of aids to support us. Two of the best are the Irish Jesuits' www.sacredspace.com, an online resource for your computer or mobile device that guides us through a session of prayer in six stages, including preparing our body and mind, and culminating in reflection on a scripture passage chosen specially for the day. It is now available in eighteen languages. The even more mobile www.pray-as-you-go.org is from the British Jesuits. It is a daily prayer session available in five languages, designed for use on MP3 players, to help us pray while traveling to and from work or school or wherever. The guided meditation with music usually runs between eleven to thirteen minutes. There are many other websites to help and support busy people reflect on God's Word. Whether it is using these new technologies, or the Liturgy of the Hours, or *lectio divina*, there is no substitute for pondering God's Word.

GATHERING WITH THE ASSEMBLY

When I do a baptism I always start by saying that for the first three hundred years of the Church's history, this sacrament was celebrated at dawn on the Easter Vigil, not only because the rising sun symbolized Christ's light dawning in our lives, but because baptism was always done in secret. For three hundred years, Christians who took the waters of baptism at dawn could be dead by lunchtime. For them, baptism was no social day out; it was a life-and-death commitment. It is on the basis of the witness of the martyrs that, generally, but not universally, we gather for public prayer in freedom and peace.

In a world increasingly hostile to religion, having and holding faith can be a very arduous business. We need each other and we are not meant to be soldiering on our own. There was a good reason Jesus left behind a community. Christ was never under any illusions about what following his lead might cost, but he underlined how much we need each other to survive in this world. And we need his protection. We often like to feel so self-sufficient these days that we bristle when we hear how Christ "protects" us, but that is precisely what he does. That protection comes through prayer, reading the Word, celebrating the sacraments, and participating in the life of the Church. Unfortunately, local Catholic assemblies can leave a little to be desired. It would be very foolish to note falling rates of practicing Catholics in every Western country of which I am aware, and blame it all on secularism. That plays its role for sure, but it has been my constant experience that good liturgy enlivens faith and bad liturgy deadens it. So what are we looking for when we come to public prayer?

A few years back there was a survey done across several English-speaking countries. They asked Catholics eighteen to thirty-five (the fastest disappearing group in the Church): What keeps you coming to Sunday Mass? The overwhelming top three responses were: 1) a warm and generous community; 2) good music and good preaching; 3) a community that practices what it preaches.

WARMTH AND HOSPITALITY OF THE COMMUNITY

One of the big issues in liturgy in the Catholic Church concerns who is welcome and who is not. Let's get really clear, the official teaching of the Church remains that only those who are in "a state of grace" can receive Holy Communion. The way some people speak about who they think are in or are not in a state of grace and therefore should or should not be receiving Holy Communion leads me to conclude that they work out of a "shape up or ship out" model of membership. The problem with this position is that it is irreconcilable with the practice of Jesus.

Toward the end of John's Gospel, we have the powerful story about how the Apostle Thomas doubts that Jesus has been raised from the dead. As a result, he is consolingly known as "doubting Thomas." If you're like me, you have believed that Thomas doubts Jesus. But let's read the story more carefully. It's not Jesus Thomas doubts, it's the disciples. In fact, when Jesus appears to them seven days later, Thomas has the opportunity to share in the experience of the Risen Lord and like the others, he immediately confesses Easter faith. Thomas' major blunder was being in the wrong place at the wrong time, and then applying a rather healthy cynicism to the disciples' seemingly ridiculous tale.

Three elements in this story should give us great comfort. The first is that Thomas doubts the early Church, and not just in regard to a minor issue of discipline or procedure. He doubts the central Christian message: that God raised Jesus from the dead. Some of us, too, at various times in our lives, can have doubts about all sorts of things in our faith. Very few Catholics get through life without asking some serious questions of God, about Jesus, the Spirit, and the Church. These questions are good in themselves. They are necessary for a mature, adult faith. What we need to ensure is that we sincerely want answers to the questions we ask and don't just use them to justify our wandering away from our faith. Thomas is the patron saint of all of us who sometimes struggle to believe what everyone else in the Church seems to accept. And he is also the patron saint of those of us who seek the courage and patience to search for the answers.

The second consoling fact in this story concerns the earliest Church. Even though they were filled with the presence of the Risen Lord and though Thomas refuses to believe their witness, they remain faithful to him in his doubts. We know this because he is still with them a week later. They didn't expel him from the group or excommunicate him; they held on to him in the hope that he would experience the Lord for himself.

I would like a dollar for every time in the last twenty years that I have been a priest that a conversation has started with "Father I used to go to Mass but," or "I used to be a Catholic but," or "I used to be a believer but…" and they go on to talk about how unwelcome they feel because of contraception, IVF, abortion, or because of being homosexual or the parents of a homosexual, being divorced and remarried, or being angry about women's leadership in the Church. What strikes me about this list is the preponderance of sexual, gender, and reproductive issues here. Why is it that I have never heard any person say they left the Church because they hate refugees, are racist, are sexist, hate gay people, are domestically violent, or refuse to share their goods with the poor? The Church's teaching is as strong and clear on these social issues as on the ones in regard to sexuality, but we often are perceived as being only really concerned about just sex, gender, and reproduction. "Jesus wept" (John 11:35).

We are welcoming and hospitable to others in God's name because God is extravagantly hospitable to us. While every group has its boundaries and there are limits from which people can dissent, we could take the earliest Church as our model and stay open to our doubters for as long as we possibly can, and so help them come to see the transforming truth that has changed our lives.

GOOD MUSIC AND GOOD PREACHING

Bishops, priests, and deacons spend a good deal of time preparing and giving homilies. But that does not mean we are good at it. A cursory glance at a seminary syllabus reveals that in nearly every case we pay less attention to the art and craft of preaching and homiletics than any other Christian denomination. The old days of thinking that a solid theological and biblical education was sufficient are over. These days, the competition for the minds, hearts, and souls of our young people is fierce indeed.

The first challenge, then, is whether we give our preachers any feedback about what they communicate—knowing that what is said and what is being communicated could be two very different things. And it works both ways. Sometimes our pastor is so loved and respected he gets away with a mediocre homily, because the best homily he gives is the way he lives. Yet while others might give great homilies, their lives do not reflect the simplicity, humility, and charity which is meant to mark out our Christians leaders.

When we come to preach, one size does not fit all, but from the gripes we constantly hear about homilies from surveys of Catholics, we know there are four problems that actually get in the way of public prayer being prayerful: they are too long; the congregation cannot understand the accent of the homilist; they are over the heads of the congregation; and they do not intersect with the assembly's daily lives.

The 2008 Synod on the Word made a few recommendations: prepare Sunday homilies nearly a week in advance; meditate upon the readings throughout the week "in light of specific events, at personal and community levels." To that end, a good homilist needs to: use both the Bible and a newspaper; determine the main theme of the homily; inspire both the hearts and intellects of the faithful; help the people to memorize the theme of the homily; prompt a concrete action such as praying, reading, or doing an activity at home, work, or in the community; and remember that in general the homily should not be longer than eight minutes, the average time listeners can concentrate.

It should never be a distraction to our prayer at liturgy if a layperson preaches. It is permitted. The 1983 Code of Canon Law, nos. 759–761, 766, say that while a homily is given by a deacon, priest, or bishop, a layperson may preach. The occasions when suitably qualified laypeople may preach are if the bishop judges it to be to the spiritual advantage of the faithful; necessity requires it; and there is a particular circumstance. In some dioceses, all of these circumstances are well and truly with us now. At the same time, however, laywomen and laymen of demonstrated faith and education should also be called to cooperate in the exercise of the ministry of the Word.

Music should follow similar lines. There is such a variation between parishes, dioceses, and countries in regard to the way music is selected and performed. Sadly, it can become a question these days of how wealthy a parish is as to how accomplished their music program is. A general rule in the English-speaking world is that the United States leads the field in the overall professionalism of its music ministry, not only because the donations are higher but also because, rightly in my opinion, the money claimed on the parish budget on music and liturgy is considered under the category of "the greatest good for the greatest number."

Many parishes used to have a heroic religious sister, often a highly trained musician, who toiled away tirelessly through the Sunday Masses and devotions with choirs and congregational hymn singing. Sister did it all for God, which left some parishes with the impression that musicians should never be paid. We never asked that of the housekeeper, secretary, accountant, or the gardener, unless they volunteered to offer their time for free. Where possible we need to hire the best musicians we can afford. It can be very difficult to pray at a public liturgy when the reader cannot read, the singer cannot sing, the organist is clearly struggling, and the preacher is not prepared.

We need to be careful of a few things. While our music and liturgy should be done with beauty and grace, we need to avoid turning our worship into a show. The liturgy is by definition a *sacred drama*. It has dramatic qualities built into it, but our prayer is better served when we are engaged, rather than entertained. Unfortunately, in the name of entertainment and the limitations of some musicians only one style or genre of music is presented and sung. Older hymns and music from our rich Catholic tradition, however, can be great vehicles of prayer. I am as worried about someone who will not sing something because "it's old hat" as much as by someone who thinks anything written after 1900 is suspect. A wide repertoire aids the greatest number for the greatest good.

The criteria for selecting good music is knowing what each part of the liturgy intends to achieve and whether this music serves that end; is the music supporting the assembly's prayer; whose need is being met by the music choice? I think some of our liturgies and music should tap into the emotional aspects to our faith much more than they do. We should have no trouble in touching the heart, but we need to avoid emotionalism, where the congregation is meant to cry on cue. Allied to this is avoiding gimmicks. The Church's liturgy when done in the way Vatican II envisaged is powerful and beautiful. Public prayer is formal and stylized. But that does not mean it has to be alienating and remote.

BEARING WITNESS TO CHRIST

If the goal of our full, conscious, and active participation in liturgical prayer is, as the Church says, to send us out to witness to Christ in the world, then we might start with our language. We use a whole range of words to describe what the earliest Christians simply called "the breaking of the bread" (Acts 2:46). *Eucharist* comes from a Greek word meaning "to give thanks." *Liturgy* is Greek too, meaning "a ritual." *Mass* is from the Latin word *missa* meaning "to be sent." So when we say we are going to Mass we are saying we are going to our commissioning to live out the Gospel in our daily or weekly lives. Therefore, every liturgy should have some element of how we are to live God's justice in the world. In the final chapter of this book, when I turn to mission and prayer, I want to deal with practicing what we preach.

Why bother praying? Public prayer matters because I am not just saved as an individual, but we are saved as the people of God. We need each other to rise to that invitation as we come together to pray in an assembly that stands before mystery in awe and wonder, is hospitable, expresses ancient faith, and works for justice right here and now. While we always celebrate what Christ is doing in the sacraments, it is also Christ who is not just in heaven but who meets us in the everyday and normal experiences of our daily lives. God's greatness meets our frailty. Now that's something to shout and sing about.

Chapter 7

Mary

In chapter four, when we were exploring the various schools of prayer in the Catholic tradition, it was clear that Mary, the Mother of God, played an important role in some of the schools. Indeed, for thousands of years Mary, first among the saints, and all the saints who have followed her, have been models of faith, companions on the journey of prayer, and support in our prayer. The martyrs were the earliest saints that were venerated. All Saints Day has its roots in the early Church's "Martyrs Day," attested to by a hymn written in 359 by St. Ephraim. Other saints and mystics of heroic virtue followed; in the seventh century the commemoration of the martyrs was called All Saints Day, and we have it as a feast to this day.

Mary's history is even more complex, as we will soon see. These days, Mary is either given too much attention—for some she can even seem to displace the Holy Spirit—or she is given next to no attention at all. It is also scandalous that except for the Orthodox, High Church Anglicans, and the Catholics, other churches have considered Mary a dividing line over the years. I think we can reclaim this long and extraordinary tradition in a way that is sane, ecumenical, inclusive, liberating, and Catholic. It is worth bothering about.

It's amazing to think that until only a few years ago, at home, at school, and in the parish and diocese we had so many devotions to Mary, and then they seemed to vanish overnight. I can remember: novenas to the Blessed Virgin Mary; the Children of Mary; the family Rosary; the rosary statue; May and October altars; scapulars; medals; sodalities; the Legion of Mary; the Teams of Our Lady; the numerous congregations of sisters, brothers, and priests named in honor of Our Lady; how many religious sisters had Mary in their names; and how some parishes had processions on various Marian feast days. Catholic kids used to get school holidays on the feast of the Assumption and the Immaculate Conception; that was among the best things about going to Catholic school.

My most affectionate and early memory of devotion to Mary was the Rosary. From the time I was eight, I spent most of my holidays at my Uncle Maurice and Aunty Claire's ranch in the outback of Australia. I come from a large extended Irish/Australian Catholic family. Maurice Leonard was the patriarch of the nine Leonard children. He used to call up each family before the school holidays and invite his nieces and nephews for the vacation. There could be up to ten cousins on holiday there at any one time. It's only now I think of Aunty Claire cooking, cleaning, and washing for that crowd.

Uncle Maurice and Aunty Claire were married in 1948. Every day until Uncle Maurice died a few years ago, they said the Rosary. And even though the nightly devotion was falling off in our homes when we were children in the 1970s, when we went to their ranch for holidays we would all kneel down after dinner and recite the five decades. Because Maurice and Claire had become so used to each other's patterns of prayer, they had a very distinctive way of "giving out" the Hail Mary and responding with the Holy Mary. Uncle Maurice would say, "Hail Mare mingum, blest la jim." By the time Maurice got to "mingum," which I assume was "among women," Claire would start "Whole may may mem." And so it went: "Hail Mare mingum, blest la jim/Whole may may mem" They were speaking in tongues long before it was trendy! If any of the cousins were too slow in actually saying "Hail Mary, full of grace…," Uncle Maurice would say, "Speed it up, Rich." So, if you can't beat 'em, join 'em, and so we all said "Hail Mare mingum, blest la jim. Whole may may mem." Of course, Claire and Maurice rightly understood that the Rosary was a mantra prayer. We are not meant to meditate on every word of every prayer but to use the words to still our minds and focus on the chapter of Jesus' life in each mystery. This is precisely what they did.

The other features of Uncle Maurice's Rosary were what he called the "toppings and tailings." These were all the prayers before and after the Rosary—do you remember them? They seemed to go on longer than the Rosary did. We said the Apostles' Creed, the Benedictus, and the Magnificat before, and then prayers to the Sacred Heart, for the conversion of Russia (that worked!), and for the protection of the pope (that worked too!).

About eighteen years on from when I started holidaying on the family ranch, I decided to enter the Jesuits. One of my other cousins, who went to that ranch as often as I did, took me out for dinner. Given what I was doing with my life, matters religious were on the agenda. Out of nowhere my cousin said across the table, "Hail Mare mingum, blest la jim" to which I immediately replied, "Whole may may mem." And back and forth it went for a while until the waiter asked us which Eastern Bloc country we came from! During the meal, we recalled lots of happy memories of those summer holidays, including saying the Rosary. At one stage my cousin said, "There was one weird prayer Uncle Maurice used to say in the "tailings," do you remember it, when he hit his chest." "What was weird about it?" I asked. "Well, it's a bit strange, don't you think, to hit your chest and call out, 'Say G'day to Jesus' and then everyone replies, 'Have Mercy on us.'" Now, this is an Australian moment, but my uncle had a very broad Australian accent. What my cousin thought was "Say G'day to Jesus" was in fact "Sacred Heart of Jesus." And at that moment I could hear my uncle saying it, and could well understand how a young boy thought his uncle was "Saying G'day to Jesus" to which we all called back, "Have mercy on us." This was a tough religion!

We have lost something important as we quickly moved away from those family practices. But it is more than possible to have a very healthy devotion to Mary as first among the saints, a companion to us in the journey of faith, a prophet, and a mother.

MARY AND THE VATICAN COUNCIL

Some people quite wrongly argue that the Second Vatican Council sidelined Our Lady. No one who goes to daily Mass could say that. The Church still has seventeen universal feasts particularly focused on Mary throughout the liturgical year which in order are:

- Mary, the Mother of God
- The Presentation of Our Lord
- Our Lady of Lourdes
- The Annunciation
- Our Lady of Fatima
- Mary, Help of Christians
- The Visitation
- The Immaculate Heart of Mary
- Our Lady of Mount Carmel
- The Assumption
- The Queenship of Mary
- The Nativity of Mary
- The Most Holy Name of Mary
- Our Lady of Sorrows
- Our Lady of the Rosary
- The Presentation of Mary
- The Immaculate Conception

What the council did in 1962 was to clean up the liturgical books that had gathered more and more saints' days and Marian feasts over the centuries. The principle of the liturgical reform was that "more is not necessarily better." Some of the feasts that were dropped were: Mary's wedding on January 23; Mary's transfiguration on August 6; and Mary's motherhood on October 11. Vatican II left it up to individual bishops to include local Marian feast days that had a direct connection with local or national devotions, and some more have been added in every country in the world.

There are a further seven feasts in which Mary is honored indirectly:

- The Presentation of the Child Jesus in the Temple
- Sts. Joachim and Ann (the parents of Mary)
- Christmas
- Epiphany
- St. Joseph, Spouse of Mary
- The Holy Family
- The Holy Innocents

Leaving aside the Saturdays where, if there are no other major feast days, then they are given over to honor Mary, there are a total of twenty-four universal feasts in the liturgical prayer of the Church in which her life and legacy are celebrated.

MARY IN THE TRADITION

To reclaim the richness of the tradition it is necessary to know it. There are libraries of books written on the outline below, but this brief summary will do for now.

In the earliest Gospel, Mark, the first mention of Mary is when Jesus rebuffs her, saying that his family is those who hear the Word of God and keep it. Mark also tells us the story of Mary being present when Jesus is rejected at Nazareth. In Luke and Matthew, Mary is the model disciple. She freely says yes to becoming the mother of Jesus, and accompanies and supports him throughout his life, death, and resurrection. Luke also records her presence at Pentecost. In John's Gospel, she is never called Mary, but the mother of Jesus, and she is with Jesus at the beginning of his public ministry at Cana, where she intercedes for the bride and groom, and at the foot of the cross, where she is given as a mother to John and the Church.

Justin Martyr, in the second century, is the first theologian whose writings we still have about Mary. Taking, of course, a literal reading of the Genesis account, he says that just as sin entered the world through Eve, so salvation has entered the world through Mary. He argued that "the woman" in Revelation 12 was Mary. Scholars these days tend to agree that "the woman" in the Book of Revelation is the Church, since she ends up the bride of Christ. In 235, Hippolytus said that Mary was sinless. At the Council of Nicea in 315, nothing was directly defined about Mary. It was called to deal with the Arian heresy, which held that Jesus was more than a man but less than God, that he was created by God. The council defined the Son as "consubstantial" with the Father: "light from light, true God from true God, begotten, not made...." Given this definition, more questions and inquiries arose in regard to Jesus and Mary.

The Council of Ephesus in 431 firmly established Mary's role in the doctrine of the Church. This council was called to refute Nestorianism, which held that the human and divine natures of Jesus were separate. The council defined that Jesus was at the same time truly human and truly divine, and went on to declare Mary to be the Theotokos, the God-carrier, which has come to be called "Mother of God." Curiously, prior to its wholesale conversion to Christianity, Ephesus was devoted to the local cult of the goddess Diana, and her preeminent title was "Stella Maris" (Star of the Sea), a title later transferred to Mary and is with us to this day. The Council of Chalcedon in 451 settled the question of Jesus' humanity and divinity by saying that he was "perfect in divinity and perfect in humanity," "like us in all things but sin." From here rose further reflections about both Jesus' and Mary's origins and conceptions.

Although some early theologians spoke of Mary being holy and pure, it was not until St. Augustine in the late fourth century that an explicit statement was made that Mary was free from original sin.

By the sixth century, in the East there was a feast of Mary's "falling asleep." The following century, the Roman Church began celebrating Mary's "dormition." It was John of Damascus who was the first to teach in his own name that Mary's body was assumed into heaven. (There is nothing in the doctrine of the assumption that says Mary did not die; only that she did not know the corruption of the grave.) By the ninth century, Syria was celebrating the Immaculate Conception as a feast day.

By the twelfth century, Bernard of Clairvaux argued that Mary has a powerful intercessory role with God in heaven. In Lyon in 1128, the Immaculate Conception was declared a feast. An interesting footnote to all this is that in the thirteenth century, St. Thomas Aquinas rejected the doctrine of the Immaculate Conception because he was anxious that it placed Mary outside the grace of redemption in Christ. In the fourteenth century, the Franciscan theologian Duns Scotus argued that the Immaculate Conception was a necessary grace of Christ given before him to prepare the way for him.

Over the next several centuries, devotion to Mary in Catholic circles reached great heights in theological development and popular piety. In 1854, Pius IX defined the teaching of the Immaculate Conception of Mary. In 1950, Pius XII defined the assumption of Mary. When the Second Vatican Council was convoked in 1962, the bishops rejected writing a freestanding document about Mary, but not because they did not have great devotion to her: they did. They wanted Mary, however, not to be aloof from the life of the Church, but integral to it, so they wrote "The Role of the Blessed Virgin Mary, Mother of God, in the Mystery of Christ and the Church" as chapter VIII of the most important document of the Council, *The Dogmatic Constitution on the Church*. It was published in 1964.

One of the things that occurs throughout the development of this doctrine is that church architecture reflects theology. As churches became bigger, taller, longer, and larger, the tabernacle went further back and the laity was forbidden to enter the sanctuary. There was a much greater emphasis on Jesus as king, ruler, and judge. Somehow, at least in the devotional life of the Church, people needed access to God. They were not worthy of the presence of the Lord. The sacraments, for example, were infrequently received. So even in the architecture of the church, as Jesus moved back, Mary came forward. Her statue or shrine was outside the altar rails, often with her own chapel halfway down the church, with ready access for the faithful. The piety that grew up over the centuries was that it was the mother of God who would hear our cries, take pity on us, and take our prayers to her Son.

Why did the great devotion to Mary almost vanish between 1968 to 1974? Because while Vatican II did not want to diminish Mary in any way, they also recovered in formula and practice a more ancient, appropriate, and central focus on our relationship with Jesus and his compassion, love, and forgiveness. In a short time, Christ was no longer aloof, distant, and to be feared. The Church teaches that the Lord will be merciful, even as judge, fully knowing our hearts. People no longer needed to go to Mary and the saints in the same way as they did to get access to the Father, Son, and Holy Spirit. They could "deal direct." We should also note that Vatican II's reclamation of the intimacy and primacy of our relationship with Christ had been building through the centuries in the various schools of prayer and, for example, in the devotion to the Sacred Heart of Jesus.

WHY BOTHER RECLAIMING MARY NOW?

First, at its best, devotion to Mary has been human, responsive, and adaptable. And it can be now. When we understand the history, dynamism, and depth of our tradition about Mary, then we see how it comes out of real communities who were asking real questions of their faith. Some of these may not be as alive or applicable today, but the way we pray with Mary does not have to drip with piety. There is nothing sentimental and pious about the Magnificat in Luke's Gospel. In this great hymn, Mary proclaims that God, through Jesus, will show strength by scattering people's pride, tear down the mighty from their thrones, and raise up in the poor in their place. God will fill the hungry and send the rich, who have not shared, away empty. In this the promise of salvation will be fulfilled for *all* people.

I think the best place from which to start a contemporary approach to Mary is to heed the advice of Paul VI in his great Marian document *Marialis Cultus* and begin with the ten episodes about Mary in the New Testament: the annunciation, the visitation, the nativity, the presentation of the child Jesus in the temple, the flight to Egypt, the losing of Jesus in the temple, when Mary goes to bring Jesus home from his public ministry, the crucifixion, and Pentecost. The religious truths contained in the scriptures cannot lead us astray in our spiritual lives, and these texts provide enough flesh and blood moments for our prayer that can intersect with our real lives. They also end up being the ways in which Mary can bring us together ecumenically.

THE ANNUNCIATION

There is nothing in our understanding of the annunciation that says Mary and Joseph were not at the normal betrothal ages for first-century Palestine, twelve to fourteen for girls, seventeen to nineteen for men. Splitting the difference, we have a pregnant thirteen-year-old and her eighteen-year-old fiancé who knows he is not the father. A teenage pregnancy is still a trauma, but in this particular circumstance, imagine the potential shame. As I have already said, Mary was not coerced to say "yes." Although singularly blest by God, she was a free human and could have said "no." That's what makes her "yes" even greater. Mary's *fiat* sets in motion the entire Christian drama. In his film *Jesus of Nazareth*, Franco Zeffirelli pictures the annunciation this way: Mary is asleep at night when a gust of wind opens a high window. Afraid at all the commotion, Mary gets up and starts to pray. As she prays, we see her face change and her body bend over. With tears in her eyes, Mary looks up through the window to the moonlit sky and simply says, "Be it done unto me as you have said." The swirling wind dies down at once. The wind here has a few other references. The word for both wind and breath in Hebrew is *ruach*, and when the wind appears in the Old Testament, often a mighty work of God follows. The wind also returns at the beginning of the Acts of the Apostles at the coming of the Holy Spirit. When the *ruach*, the wind, and the Spirit are afoot, creation and re-creation abound. For us, too, the annunciation is an opportunity to reflect on what God has done for us in Jesus Christ, and to enter more deeply into the mystery of who God is calling us to be right now. In what ways do I let Christ be born in me? And in what ways do I need Christ to be born in me?

THE VISITATION

The tradition has not been kind to St. Elizabeth. She is always made out to be ninety-nine. Religious art has not helped.

Given that in Jesus' day most people were dead by fifty (that's why three score and ten is such a colossal age), Elizabeth would have been old at thirty-six and may have been going through menopause, during which she became pregnant, not an unknown occurence to this day. But the visitation is one of the most moving scenes in the Gospel. On a human level here are two cousins, both unexpectedly pregnant in the most extraordinary circumstances, meeting and offering each other greetings and support. We can see the scene and feel the bond. They meet in the mountains (the hill country) where God has always been manifest to the Israelites. Elizabeth embodies the Old Covenant made to Israel and she carries John who will be the herald of the Messiah. Mary embodies the new, and final, covenant in Jesus. Elizabeth recognizes what is happening here and she embraces all that God is doing for the world. She has tasted the promise of God and now sees its fulfilment.

THE NATIVITY

Do you know how far it is to walk from Nazareth to Bethlehem? About 100 miles (160 kms), and we are told that Mary does this on the back of the donkey in the last weeks of her pregnancy. No wonder she has Jesus within minutes of arriving! Jesus did not come in a palace as a prince. He was born in a cave where the smell of animals must have been shocking. This is far from the sanitized image we have on our Christmas cards or of which we sing in our carols. This is Emmanuel, God meeting us as we are and leading us to find the way to a life that has meaning and purpose, preparing us for eternal life. The Nativity says that God is okay with mess.

As an enjoyable aside, let me tell you about the best nativity play I have ever seen. In 1994, I was invited by an elderly nun to be the guest of honor at the Sacred Heart Primary School's nativity play in Melbourne. The school is a great mix of children from the wealthier inner-city terrace houses and from the high-rise housing projects. That year it was the turn of the third grade (eight years of age) to perform the play.

When I arrived, Sister told me that she had trouble with the boy who was playing the innkeeper because he had his heart set on playing St. Joseph. "He is an Islamic boy and I really thought I should at least have a Christian, if not a Catholic, boy playing St. Joseph." Rehearsals had not gone well, but she was sure everything would be fine in the performance.

The whole school was there along with all the parents of the third grade. In the front row of the school hall was the principal, Sister, and me.

As Mary and Joseph knocked on the makeshift wall that was the inn's door, the innkeeper gruffly yelled out, "Who's there?" "I am Joseph and this is my wife Mary and we have nowhere to stay tonight and she is having a baby." (Having a baby? If her baby bump was anything to go by, that girl was having octuplets!) The innkeeper did not budge. Sister leaned forward and in a loud stage whisper said, "Ahmed, you know what to do, darling. You know your lines. Open the door and make your very important speech." He didn't budge.

So Sister told Joseph to knock again. The innkeeper barked more angrily, "Who's there?" We got Joseph's speech again, but the little innkeeper didn't move. The tension was rising in that room now, so Sister leaned forward again and in a stronger voice said, "Ahmed, your Mum and Dad are here, darling, and they will be so proud of you. Now just play your part and make us all proud." Sister then told Joseph to knock for the third time, and he gave out his speech again. Now before Ahmed could decide what to do next, a loud African bass voice came from the back of the room, "Ahmed, you open that goddamn door or I'll belt your bum!" I turned around to see the tallest human being I have ever seen. Ahmed's father, Mohammed, was a refugee to Australia from

Sierra Leone. He was six feet eight inches tall and told me he weighed in at 238 pounds (107 kg.) of solid body mass. So proud was he that his son had a starring role in the Christmas play that he was dressed in his magnificent white celebratory kaftan with a small white cap on his head. Now, however, he was coming down the aisle toward the stage, and every adult there was thinking, "Open the door, open the door, open the goddamn door, because I think your bum belted by this guy is going to hurt." Someone intercepted Mohammed as Ahmed opened the door and said plaintively to Mary, "You can come in," but then shouted at Joseph, "but you can piss off!" With that, Joseph burst into tears, the shepherds and the three wise men started a fight with the innkeeper "because he said a rude word," and Sister stood up, turned to everyone, and said, "This wasn't the way it was supposed to go." It took ten minutes to restore peace.

It was the best nativity play I have ever seen. God is good with mess.

THE PRESENTATION OF THE CHILD JESUS IN THE TEMPLE

This event tells us what devout Jews the Holy Family was. They did everything prescribed by the Law which, in this case, stipulated that forty days after a child's birth the parents should present their baby in the temple as an act of thanksgiving. As we have seen, forty is a time for formation. Here we meet Simeon and Anna, who foretell that just as the Israelites entered the Promised Land after forty years in the desert, so now the time of waiting, of formation, is over. Israel can receive the promised Messiah. How do we make this moment our own? We present ourselves in prayer knowing that God is intimately familiar with us. It is crazy that we should be anything but ourselves before him. But we sometimes go through the pretence of dressing things up, pretending otherwise, or putting on a show.

THE FLIGHT INTO EGYPT

On every level this is one of the most terrifying stories in the Gospel. Only Matthew relates it and I think it is a theological story more than a factual one. At least I hope so. Not because Jesus is not saved from a tyrant. So far so good. But what about all the other babies who were slaughtered? Didn't God care about them too? What were they, collateral damage? Alternatively, Matthew is beginning to draw his picture of Jesus as the new Moses. Just as Moses was saved as a child and goes to Egypt, so is Jesus, but with even more drama. By the end of the Gospel, just as Moses gave the Law, Jesus *is* the Law. At center of this dramatic story is Herod, who is locked in fear. Matthew will later portray Pilate in a similar way. The result of being threatened by who Jesus is, or how he lives his life, results in death—Herod's slaughter of the innocents in the first case, and later Pilate's capital punishment of Jesus. Matthew tells us that the enemy of the Christian life is fear, so this event in our prayer is a moment to take flight from our fear and embrace freedom.

THE LOSING OF JESUS IN THE TEMPLE

Have you ever lost your children in a department store? That frantic terrible search—and the longer the search goes on, the more fear builds. So much so, that when you find your children you want to love them and murder them in the same instant. There are so many delicious details in this story. Jesus is twelve (the fulfillment of Israel) when the holy family goes up to Jerusalem and loses the boy on the way home. It took them days to realize they had lost him. These days Mary and Joseph would be reported to the Department of Children Services. But they found him on the third day (the work of the Lord), teaching the scribes—another new Moses moment in Matthew's Gospel. And they did not understand why he had done this to them. I know a few mothers and fathers who can empathize with that.

MARY GOES TO BRING JESUS HOME FROM HIS PUBLIC MINISTRY

This most curious of stories is not often read at liturgies. I am sure the Christian Family Association will not be having it at their annual Mass! But Jesus is creating a stir in the district and so Mary and his family go to bring him home. This gives consolation to a parent who cannot really work things out with his or her children, what path they are taking, and where it will end.

THE CRUCIFIXION

Imagine what it is like to watch your child undergo capital punishment. That's what Mary does. And just to bring it home some more, imagine Jesus did not die on the cross. We have domesticated that image a little too much. Imagine he died in the electric chair, was shot by firing squad, or was given a lethal injection, his mother watching the whole event, unable to do a thing about it. Praying here with Mary is about all those moments in life that are criminally and horribly unfair, when we are powerless to stop them. Mary has something to say to any parent who has ever lost a child in death, before or after they were born.

PENTECOST

In the last chapter I mentioned that in Luke/Acts it is fifty days from Easter Day to Pentecost and fifty is the number of the jubilee when the slaves are set free, the fields are allowed to go fallow, and debts are forgiven. Here is Mary in the center of the earliest Church as it starts its mission in Christ's name to set people free, to reap a new harvest, and to declare that humanity is debt-free.

Even these few reflections on Mary's role in the life of Jesus enable us to let go of a plaster statue and be accompanied by a flesh-and-blood woman: mother, sister, saint, prophet, and friend. To reclaim our prayer to and with her, it is good to be reminded that she was fully and truly human. Mary is not God. She needed God's redemption in Christ and this poor, simple Jewish woman is the pre-eminent disciple of the kingdom Jesus proclaimed. She has something to say to anyone in our world who is a teenage mother, a poor, hard-working, religious person, a refugee, and a so-called person of color. Like Jesus, Mary was not white. She gives consolation to parents who can't understand their children, have ever lost a child in a marketplace, or been through the heartbreak of losing a child in death.

MARIAN DOGMAS

These days it can be especially difficult to talk to young people about the main Marian dogmas: the Immaculate Conception and the assumption. Parents and teachers have told me that their teenagers and young adults can look at them with confident incredulity and say, "Do you really believe all that stuff?" They may be happy to take these doctrines on board in a symbolic or poetic way, but not in the way the Church actually teaches them.

THE IMMACULATE CONCEPTION

It must be conceded that the circumstances around the conception of Mary and the birth of Jesus are in line with other extraordinary birth narratives found in the mythologies of Zoroaster, Isis and Horus, Marduk, Oannes, Hercules, Pan, and to a lesser extent Moses and Isaac. The Immaculate Conception is about Mary's conception, not Jesus' (that's the annunciation). While it is has a very long history in Christian faith, it emerges strongly in its own right when the early Church was trying to formulate how it understood Jesus to be God and a human being. As God, Jesus could not be born of a sinful human being, so this doctrine was established to say that God prepared the way for the coming of the Lord.

At its simplest level, the Immaculate Conception says that God does homework. Mary was not invited to be the mother of Jesus without any preparation. Mary was given the requisite gifts for her mission. Though of a vastly different order, we can see that from our conception, too, we have all received certain gifts from God. Some of us have the potential to be brilliant musicians, academics, sports men and women, or we have the innate courage to become campaigners for justice, development, and peace. By nature and grace, God prepares all of us to change our world for the better.

Like a musician, an athlete, a sportsperson, or a campaigner for human rights who realizes his or her full potential in this life, Mary went on to realize the fullness of the unique spiritual gifts she was given. And, like some of us who strive to achieve perfection in our particular areas, we know it comes at a cost.

As anyone who has read *Where the Hell Is God?* will know, I do not have strong belief in an interventionist God. I think, generally, God works in and through the natural and human processes he has set in place. But if we are going to believe that God took human flesh in the incarnation, then that is already a most dramatic intervention in the world, indeed, the definitive intervention. To say God did some homework in preparation for that moment makes sense. Who wouldn't? We have already said that Mary, however, was not coerced into saying yes. She was invited. To a lesser but still important degree, so are we.

THE ASSUMPTION

Here it must also be acknowledged that religious mythologies have stories about assumptions and ascensions: Peshotanu,

Hercules, Apolloniys of Tyana, Yudhishthira, Sant Tukaram, Chaitanya Mahaprabhu, Swami Ramalinga, Muhammad, Mahdi, Enoch, and in some non-canonical texts, even Moses ascended to heaven after his death.

While the doctrine of the assumption is a singular gift granted to Mary for her singular fidelity to Jesus her Son, it tells us that it is possible for humanity to be assumed into God. I find it especially heartening that the dogma also says that Mary's assumption gives us all hope because her "assumption into heaven will make our belief in our own resurrection stronger and render it more effective." So, again at its simplest, God will remain faithful to us as we are faithful to God. And while not understating the special honor Mary received, the assumption prefigures the joy of union with God that, one day, can be ours in the life to come if we remain faithful as well.

MARIAN APPARITIONS

In the last hundred years, claims of apparitions of Mary have occurred in nearly ninety places. The Church only officially recognizes ten as "worthy of belief": Guadalupe, Mexico; Laus, France; Rue du Bac, Paris, France; La Salette, France; Lourdes, France; Pontmain, France; Fatima, Portugal; Beauraling, Belgium; Banneaux, Belgium; and Akita, Japan.

I was never told this as child, but the Church actually takes a very tough stand against apparitions. In fact, in 1978 the Vatican produced a document called *The Norms Regarding the Manner of Proceeding in the Discernment of Presumed Apparitions or Revelations*. It says that most alleged apparitions are false and that over the centuries there have been a "countless number" of reported apparitions that have been proved wrong. Even if the Church says that an apparition may be "worthy of belief," that does not guarantee that the apparition actually occurred as reported. It is not sinful to disbelieve in an apparition if the Church has said an apparition is "worthy of belief," but everyone is encouraged to be respectful of it.

So we can be Catholics in full and true standing with the Church and not believe in one of them. Apparitions are private revelations that emerge from the religious experiences of mystics. On occasion, what is revealed there reinforces the Church's belief, but that is very different from endorsing the apparition itself. The Church is generally very slow to believe any of the so-called revelations that emerge from apparitions unless they state what we already believe.

Some people find the apparitions very helpful, and the sites themselves have become holy places of pilgrimage, but we need to be clear that these things are not essential for our prayer, faith, or salvation. One of my four dictums on prayer applies strongly here: *If it helps, do it; if it doesn't, don't.*

MOTHER OF THE POOR

I want to finish this chapter by relating a personal story about when my own devotion to Mary re-entered my adult life. Firstly, however, I need to tell you that when I was in grade four of my Catholic School, Sr. Mary Wenceslaus, RSM, was our music teacher. She came into class one day and taught us the twelfth-century Latin prayer to Our Lady, *Salve Regina*. Hold that thought.

On August 15, 1975, eight members of a village in the mountain country well above the capital of Chile were arrested by the military police. They were accused of being terrorists and organizing labor unions. They were innocent of the former and proudly guilty of the latter. For months, the villagers tried to find out where the men had gone and why they had been taken away. As we now know, abduction, torture, and illegal imprisonment were daily realities for Chilean people under General Pinochet.

Word arrived in November that the corpses of the parish councillors could be found in Santiago's morgue. My friend, Sr. Catherine, was an Australian nun working in that parish. She took the mothers of the eight men to the morgue in Santiago. Catherine later wrote to me, "Richard, you could not imagine what we found in the morgue. There were over 100 corpses piled high on each other and our mothers had to roll someone else's son over in an attempt to find her own. And as the mothers searched, they began to weep loudly realizing how evil we can be toward one another. As they wept, they prayed the Rosary. As one mother, and then another, found her son, they called out more desperately, 'Holy Mary, Mother of God pray for us sinners now, and at the hour of our death.'"

Catherine's letter continued, "For years I rejected devotion to Mary because I felt oppressed by the way generations of men in the Church presented her—blue veils, white skin, always smiling, a perpetual virgin and yet also a mother, an ideal I could never achieve, but one to which I was told I should aspire. In the experience of the village mothers, however, the distortions of who Mary was for a poor and suffering world faded away. Far from feeling distant from their devotion, I found myself praying with them, knowing that Mary was with us in our shock, anger, and grief."

The letter went on, "What happened next was indescribable. Twenty soldiers stood by and watched nine women load eight corpses into my truck. They never lifted a finger to help us. We could only get seven out of the eight in the back so one of the mothers cradled her son in her arms in the front with me. The journey took four hours. On the long trip home, we prayed the Rosary again and again. As the mother next to me said, 'We pray with Mary at times like this because she knows what it's like to bring a child into the world and claim his dead body in her arms.' And there it was, right beside me for the four-hour

trip into the mountains. Something changed in me for the better that day."

Twelve years later, in 1989, Catherine died of hepatitis in that village. Her family had been trying to get her to come home for months, but she lied about how ill she was and said that she had everything she needed there. The only consolation Catherine's family got was when a letter arrived from the mothers in the village. When I had it translated from Spanish into English, it read:

> We want you to know that we were with Catherine when she died. We would never have let her die alone for she was one of our children too. We often prayed the Rosary with her. She seemed to like that, thumbing the beads she used ever since she brought us back with our boys. We have buried her next to our sons and put on her tombstone the line she asked us to inscribe, "Mary, my friend, my companion, and mother of the poor, pray for me."

In 2010, I was the first member of Catherine's family or friends to go to Chile. I caught a bus from Santiago, and nearly five hours later alighted at two p.m. The five surviving mothers were waiting for me. They took me immediately to the cemetery, and there I found Catherine's grave, in among eight men who were killed in 1975. There was the inscription on her grave in English and Spanish. We all stood and wept. Then one of the women asked me to pray. They knew very little English. All I could say in Spanish was, "*Lo siento, no hablo español.*" But then like a good steward who brings out of the storehouse both things new and old, I remembered Sr. Mary Wenceslaus. By the end of that ancient love song, we were all singing and crying and hugging.

Why bother praying with Mary and the saints? Because I need all the help I can get. Now is not the time to throw out devotion to Mary, but to reclaim a relationship with her as prophet, friend, and companion in faith. If we are in touch with the facts of her life and how we came to have what we have now in our tradition, and are poor enough in spirit, then that's where the mother of the poor meets us and gently leads us to her Son.

Chapter 8

Prayer for Mission

In a previous chapter, I wrote that over recent centuries we often said that the reason we prayed was to "save our soul" or to "get to heaven." Although we might couch this in different terms today, this has not changed. But we have added to it, and rightly so. While the Gospels are clear about attaining heaven, they are equally strong about bringing heaven to bear on this world right here and now. For prayer to really take off, we need both wings. Prayer that is overly focused on otherworldly concerns is not in touch with daily life. It can quickly become formalism. Prayer that has too much emphasis on this world, without an eye on the next, can become a political campaign with no sense that even if we fall short of establishing the reign of God here, then the full realization of Christ's kingdom still awaits us.

The reason Christians seek to encounter the presence of God and maintain an intimate and loving relationship with him is because we are on mission: Christ's mission. In what is called the Great Commission, Matthew 28:18–20, Jesus sends out his disciples to continue the world he established. "All authority in heaven and on earth has been given to me. Go therefore and make disciples of all nations, baptizing them in the name of the Father and of the Son and of the Holy Spirit, and teaching them to obey everything that I have commanded you. And remember, I am with you always, to the end of the age."

Note well what Jesus did *not* say. He did not say to wait at home until the world comes to you, talking your talk and walking your walk. In Western societies, we have become very used to the world coming to us on our (the Church's) terms. It is understandable. The numbers were so large for so long that our most urgent sense of being on mission with Christ was gaining converts so we could assure them of getting to heaven. I knew a Jesuit priest who used to ask everyone he met, "Are you a Catholic?" and if the response was in the negative he would quickly follow it up with, "but I am sure you would like to be." It did the trick in starting countless spiritual conversations. As good a mission as it remains to invite people into the life of the Church, it is clear from the way Jesus lived that he also had a broader agenda for us and his mission as well.

GOING OUT TO THE REAL WORLD AS SINFUL CHURCH

When we pray to be on mission, I think we need to own that these days one of the greatest obstacles to people coming to praise, reverence, and serve God in the Church is the Church itself. Because the Lord sends us out to the real world, not the world we would prefer to evangelize, we need to listen very carefully to the fact that in the religious census or surveys in every Western democracy in the world right now, the fastest growing groups are those who do not believe in God, or do not want to belong to any religion or church.

Another interesting group are the fellow travelers I call "cultural Catholics." This is where the Church still has very high numbers of people who freely and knowingly say they are Catholic, but do not participate in any way in the life of the Church. Maybe they come for Christmas. In the United States, they might race into the church for ashes on the first day of Lent. But they are not there at Easter, those numbers are falling, and it is no longer just for baptism, marriages, and funerals (hatching, matching, and dispatching as it's sometimes called). In Western countries, those ceremonies are decreasing, and civil naming, marrying, and burying rites have risen exponentially in the last twenty years. Belonging to the Church is tribal, a cultural definition in a similar way to some branches of Judaism where someone will proudly say they are Jewish, but they do not keep a kosher kitchen or observe the dietary laws, rarely keep the Sabbath, sparingly attend synagogue, and do not mark the High Holy Days. So there is precedent for what might be emerging in Western Catholicism.

As I have said in chapter six, simply blaming "secularism" for the lack of traction the Church now has on an increasing number of people's minds and hearts, especially those under forty, is self-serving and limited. This is tough language for a tough situation. Most Western countries are now mission fields and we need to take it seriously. Not that we should be surprised that we have a hostile environment within which to preach and live the Gospel. The tradition of the Church is that almost everyone who received the Lord's Great Commission died a martyr's death, so he and they were under no illusions about the cost of discipleship. These days we have to enter into the public square, with no special status or favors, and be judged on the qualities of our arguments and the goodness of our actions. And there is the rub.

Without question, the sexual abuse crisis has been the single largest contributor to people losing confidence in the Church, withdrawing from the practice of their faith, or being confirmed in their worst judgments about us. No matter what good we do—more on that soon—the most regular reply to any good news is, these days, "yes, but what about the sexual abuse of children and its cover-up." It does not seem to help to tell the truth: that the most common place for a child to be sexually or physical abused remains the family home, up to 85 percent of all cases; that the least-reported and prosecuted cases of sexual abuse, because of cover up, are in families; that the rate of offenders among celibate males in the Catholic Church is almost identical to rate of offending males in the population as a whole; and that at least 96 percent of all priests and male religious have not had any substantiated allegations of abuse made or upheld against them. These points are not excuses. There are no excuses. They go some way to placing a context around these crimes and they counter the argument that celibacy alone is the cause of the abuse, and that all priests are to be held in suspicion as abusers or potentially so.

We have a lot to pray for in this regard. Joining some very senior people in the Church, we urgently need to bother praying for the courage to change a defensive self-interest that puts our so-called "good name" and the protection of our property and monies ahead of the just rights and claims of the victims. We have to deconstruct a clerical culture that thrives on a lack of transparency and secrecy. We need our leaders, and maybe all of us, to undertake some very significant acts of public penance over a long period of time, to embody the pain and hurt the Church has caused through what individuals have done, and what the institution has failed to do. We have to demand that the officials who exercise power in the Church, any power, be accountable for it, and are seen to be so. We have to uphold vigorously zero tolerance and mandatory reporting while being as transparent as we can be to all law enforcement agencies. Recognizing that compensation and public apologies may be necessary, they are considered by many as inconsequential. Will it cost us much more to respond fully—on every level? Yes, but not doing so will be at the expense of the service of the Gospel and the mission of the Church.

We must also live and proclaim a tough truth: that while our first instinct and action must always be for the needs and rights of the victims, we must work to forgive and reconcile the abusers as well, not to the victims, but to the community whose trust they have so deeply betrayed. We need to witness to the world what St. Augustine said in the fifth century: forgiveness is like a mother who has two wonderful daughters named justice and compassion. The forgiveness of criminals is often unpopular, but to do anything less is not worthy of Jesus Christ.

KNOWING WHAT WE ARE DOING AND WHERE WE ARE HEADED

In the Ignatian school of prayer, we are encouraged to get clear about for what or for whom we are praying. Given that intention defines the moral act, then we need to clarify how our prayer informs our mission, what that mission is, and what we expect to come from it. When we look at the Church's documents on mission, and here I am referring primarily to *Gaudium et Spes*, *Evangelii Nuntiandi*, *Redemptoris Missio*, and *Mysterium Ecclesiae*, there are three strong features about our mission to the contemporary world. We're called to proclaim the Gospel through witness, inculturation, and liberation.

WITNESS

Christian witness has two component parts, one much more important than the other: what we say and what we do. For all the complexities of philosophy and theology, the Christian message is a relatively simple one: to be a follower of Jesus we have to love God, love our neighbor, and love ourselves. I am sometimes amused by some Catholic parents who are angry because their children attend CCD or a Catholic school and say, "but they don't know the Ten Commandments." I am all for them knowing the Ten Commandments, that famous summary of the hundreds of Mosaic laws given by God to the chosen people, but it is Jesus himself who says that all religious law can be fulfilled if we love God, neighbor, and self. Love of self has had a mixed history in the Christian story, but it is essential for prayer and mission, and not just because Jesus said it. Self love is often confused with self adoration. Nothing could be further from what Jesus is saying. If we have no sense of our own self-worth, our own dignity, and the personal love God has for each of us, it is impossible for us to give the same to others and to claim from others the dignity we deserve. We will either treat others as our inferiors on the one hand, or allow others to walk all over us, on the other. Love of self is not about canonizing a loss of self-control. Jesus shows us by the way he loved his Father, us, and himself that true love always involves sacrifice. If we love ourselves in the right way, we have the self-control to forgo those things that are most destructive in our lives, and we have the generosity to do for others the things that will enrich their lives. Jesus knew that we can never love others if we hate ourselves.

If we are witnessing by the words we use, we have to get the basic message right, because words define reality.

When St. Francis Xavier, arguably the Church's greatest missionary, left Rome for Portugal and then on to India, St. Ignatius Loyola gave him one piece of advice about how to use words: "Wherever you go, learn the language." It's hard work to learn a language, especially at an advanced age, but the understanding and ease it gives within a culture amply reward the efforts involved. In many Western democracies, there is a post-modern, post-Christian language emerging now, and if we want to influence it for good then we have to adapt our words. That doesn't mean we have to water down our message. It means we have to be prudent about when we speak, what we say, and how we say it. Prudence is not one of the cardinal virtues of St. Thomas Aquinas for nothing. For public consumption, Jesus almost always used the parable, understanding that most important lessons could be learned through stories—while people are laughing, crying, being confronted, and being consoled. He also knew the art of communicating his message simply. In some respects, the Church has become too complex and serious for its own good.

Sometimes, however, it must be admitted that our religious words can easily be misunderstood. Like the young priest who was having trouble with his sermons, so he asked the bishop for help. "Well," said the bishop, "you might start with something to get the congregation's attention, such as, 'Last night I was in the warm embrace of a good woman.' I've always found that sparks their interest and then you can go on to talk about how warm and accepting she was and at the end reveal she was your mother. It's great for sermons about family love." The young priest decided to take the advice the following Sunday, but he was so nervous, something got lost in translation. He started, "Last night…I…I…I was in the warm embrace of a hot woman." The congregation audibly gasped, the young priest paused and realized he had forgotten how the bishop's story ended, so he said, "I don't remember who she was but the bishop really recommended her."

Given that the words matter, then our actions matter tenfold more. For example, the Church has not been roundly condemned for what we are saying in the sexual abuse crisis as much as for what we have done, or not done. We once thought that the only activity we needed to do was to say our prayers and go to Mass. But as Rev. Dr. Billy Graham once said, "Going to church no more makes you a Christian than living in a garage would make you a car." Dr. Graham and I agree that going to church is an essential expression of the Christian life, but we can pray incessantly and go to Mass all day and every day, and if it does not affect our relationships, our ethics, our workplaces, and our families for the better, then we are wasting our time. Rather than Christian witnesses, we could be in danger of being seen as frauds, and the world does not need more of them.

In Luke's Gospel, the teaching that immediately precedes the giving of the Lord's Prayer is all about how we act, the now famous Good Samaritan story, which is told in response to the question, "Who is my neighbor?" The Church is outstanding in responding to our neighbors, but you would be forgiven for not knowing it—because we never tell anyone—not even each other! This is a false humility.

What follows is the good the Australian Catholic Church does every day in my country. I use it because it is the scenario I know best. These statistics took me twelve months to put together. It is a good challenge to imagine a similar list for your own area, country, or denomination. But first, some background. Australia has a population of 21.5 million on a vast desert island which, if superimposed onto the United States, would go from Los Angeles to New York and from Churchill, Canada to Mexico City. In European terms it goes from Lisbon to Moscow, from the top of Scotland to Algeria. In the last census there were 5,439,268 Catholics, or 25.3 percent of the population (down from 25.8 percent in 2006). We have been the largest religious denomination in Australia for the last twenty-seven years. The second largest group is those with no religion or those who refused to answer the optional religious question on the national census. They account for 4.7 million Australians or 22.3 percent of the population, a growth of 3.6 percent since the last census five years ago.

In this context, the Australian Catholic goes on mission every day.

EDUCATION

SCHOOLS
- 713,000 children are taught in Catholic schools.
- There are 1,710 Catholic schools.

- 82,000 staff work in Catholic schools.
- There are at least 3,200 CCD volunteer teachers every week.

UNIVERSITIES

- The Australian Catholic University is the fastest growing truly national university in Australia. It has 22,932 students, an increase of 42 percent over the last three years. It has the largest number of nursing and teaching graduates in the country.
- The Notre Dame Australia won the Kullari Award for the most successful university at achieving indigenous student graduations.

HEALTH CARE

HOSPITALS

- There are sixty-six Catholic hospitals in Australia, with 9,500 beds (12 percent of all hospital beds), including nineteen public hospitals for the poor.

AGED CARE

In addition, there are:

- 22,872 residential aged care beds
- 5,393 retirement and independent living units and serviced apartments
- Eight dedicated hospices with palliative care services

WELFARE

CATHOLIC SOCIAL SERVICES

- CSS has sixty-three member organizations in Catholic Welfare Australia.
- 1.1 million clients were cared for in 2011.
- The Society of St. Vincent de Paul is the largest volun-

teer welfare network in the country, with 18,209 members and 30,910 volunteers.

AID

- Caritas Australia raised $43 million for the poor in 2010.
- Catholic Mission raised $18 million for the poor in 2010.

PARISHES

There are 1,321 Catholic parishes:

- 5.4 million Catholics
- 624,000 worship every Sunday

Most of my compatriot Catholics would not know any of this, so in our prayer we can become very discouraged. Even when these facts are presented to some people to give some balance to all the justifiably bad news stories about the Church, they will still say, "Yes, but what about sexual abuse?" Who can blame them? All that most people hear about churches, religions, and faith in the public square each day is bad news because we do not communicate these facts to our own and the wider community. It is not a question of these canceling out the crimes and shame of what has happened in recent years; rather, it is the good spirit who helps us see that the bad-news story is not the only story, and that as weak and sinful as we are, our witness by action is already there, every day, in season and out of season. I think we need to bring it into the light, not to glorify ourselves, but to "boast in the Lord," to highlight that this is what Christ the teacher, the healer, the one who raises up the poor and is the Good Shepherd achieves in and through us.

This incomplete survey is a very mixed bag. My country is a mission territory with many cultural Catholics and a dramatically rising group of people who have no interest in religion at all. Do you know the comparable statistics for the Church in your own country? The best prayer is always rooted in reality and so knowing the facts as we go out with Christ to the world is pivotal to what our prayer while on mission is all about. There are lots of good-news stories too.

INCULTURATION

When our prayer sends us out to witness by word and deed, we better know who we are, who we are going to, and what the place is like wherein we will be witnessing. These things are tasks of an inculturated faith. The first thing about an inculturated faith is that it is centered on Jesus. This is so obvious, and yet it is so critical. If we have no loving relationship with Jesus, then we have no reason to be on his mission, no frame of personal experience through which we can process our membership of the Church. But Jesus is rarely the problem. Most people like Jesus, they like what he says, and they like what he did. The Church can be the deal-breaker. But we would not have access to Jesus and his teachings that we do if we did not have the New Testament, which emerged out of the lived tradition of the people of God in the Church. If the Church is on mission, then inculturation demands that we know to whom we are sent. We have to face up to our national and world culture as it is, not as we would like it to be. We cannot be on mission to a culture we do not know or one that we simply despise. Jesus himself lived in a kingdom that was a client-state of a brutal imperial power. Palestine was, on the whole, a desperately poor country. There were significant religious divisions as well, whose leaders were hostile to Jesus' message. Yet, as nearly every page of the Gospels tells us, Jesus knew his audience and so should we. Why is it, for example, that at every evangelization conference I have ever attended we start out talking about the Church, ourselves, when I think we should start talking about the world to whom we are sent to proclaim the Gospel?

Here again, simply for familiarity, I will use Australia as a case study. The challenge remains for you to draw up a similar pen picture for your own country or area.

The "average" Australian:

- is thirty-seven years old and growing older;
- will live until they are 81.9 years old;
- lived with his or her spouse before marriage;
- is in a registered marriage (49.2 percent);
- got married at thirty by a civil marriage celebrant;
- most probably will not divorce;
- has 1.9 (increasingly unbaptized) children;
- brings home $1,234 per week;
- lives in a city (89 percent);
- lives in one of the largest houses we have ever built;
- has a monthly mortgage payment of $1,800 or weekly rent of $285;
- loses $931 a year gambling;
- donates $207 to charity;
- has someone in their family who is chronically depressed or suffers from social depression;
- watches sports, sitcoms, and so-called "reality" and "lifestyle" programs;
- has ready access to soft or hardcore pornography, an industry estimated to be worth $500 million in 2011 ($31,000 per adult);
- reads *The Australian Women's Weekly*, *Woman's Day*, and *New Idea*;
- states they are Christian (61.1 percent) but is actually un-churched, and increasingly of no religion at all;
- has 1.7 cars per household; and in addition—

- 9.5 percent live in an unregistered common law marriage;
- 41.3 percent are not married;
- 70.32 percent were born in Australia, 20.5 percent are indigenous Australians;
- 24.6 percent were born overseas: 5.3 percent from the UK, 4.8 percent from New Zealand, 1.07 percent from India, and 1.01 percent from China.

I would be very confident that, with some significant localized differences, many of these descriptors would be similar in most other Western democracies.

LIBERATION

To complement our witness in word and deed, and our inculturated faith which attends to the real world with realistic expectations of what we can do for those to whom we are sent, the Church says that our mission should also be about liberation—setting people free so that they might have the freedom of the sons and daughters of God.

When we hear the word *liberation*, we sometimes think of liberation theology, where the demands of the Gospel call us to actual social and political action to make the world a more just place. The liberation we seek could be that in some circumstances, but chances are it will be to continue what the Church is doing well already: the very best education, healthcare, welfare, and pastoral care we can possibly provide. For centuries, these have been effective instruments of opting for the poor and the marginalized, and of humanizing and creating consciences in the wealthy and the powerful. We have to re-double out efforts in these regards.

INFORMING OUR PRAYER FOR MISSION

Our mission to the world must be marked by what St. Thomas Aquinas calls in Book II of the *Summa Theologica* the cardinal virtues: justice, temperance, fortitude, and prudence. These gifts enable us to interact with a complex world, discern where the best of a culture might be, have the courage to confront those cultural elements that are dehumanizing, develop excellence of character, and chart the process by which we make careful choices.

Allied to them is how our prayer is challenged to cultivate the concrete application of these virtues in our mission to liberate.

The first is to be as compassionate toward others as Jesus is toward us. That doesn't mean we have to abandon our principles and beliefs; it means that in judging the world we should pray to see it as God sees it. I am convinced sometimes it is not what some men and women in the Church say in the public square, it is how they say it, the attitude they bring to bear, and the way they can appear to condemn anyone who disagrees with them.

Compassion also asks everyone in the Church to imagine in prayer what it's like to be a person of color, a refugee, a victim of domestic violence, gay, lesbian, or transgendered, divorced and remarried, or a person with disabilities. In our mission to set others free when we catch ourselves jumping to an immediate condemnation of someone, let's stop and pray that our first response might be, "What must life be like for you?" At that point, our mission to them will be touching on the divine.

Second, we need to liberate people from some frightening theology about where the God of love fits into a world of pain and suffering. I will not detail what I outlined in *Where the Hell Is God?* except to say that the reception to that book indicates that this question is vital in our prayer and mission. What do we say to people in the worst of times to lift the burden and ease the pain? We do not believe that God created us as playthings, brought into being for God's amusement. We do not hold that God sends episodes of pain, illness, and disease as punishment for our sins. We do believe that God made woman and man as a self-expression of divine and undeserved love. God made the universe and everything in it, not out of divine need but out of desire for our happiness. We are meant to grow and develop and have our being in God's creation. To safeguard us against feeling like pawns, God enabled the gifts of consciousness and free will to evolve so we can make choices—opening up even the possibility of our choosing against God. I did not solve the problem of evil in my book. No one has, but I am delighted that it started a conversation so that our words and actions in the world always point to hope.

Third, our prayer and mission should be marked by joy. My friend and Jesuit brother James Martin, SJ, has explored how central this theme is in the Christian life in his book *Between Heaven and Mirth*. Personally, I have lost count of how many parents and grandparents say to me, "Father, my children (or grandchildren) do not practice their faith. What am I going to do?" To which I always reply, "The most important thing you can do has nothing to do with what you should say, but the joy with which you live your life. You may not be around to see it, but I have been at wakes where unchurched family members lament that they are lacking the joy that their mother or father found in their faith. That can be the beginning of something wonderful."

There are real challenges, too, in the way priests welcome people at Mass, and at baptisms, weddings, and funerals. I am appalled every time I hear about how a priest began a packed Christmas Mass by berating the congregation for actually turning up, "because why aren't you here every week?" Why would they return? Why not thank them for coming, welcome them home for Christmas, and at the end invite them to come back any week, every week?

Furthermore, before we spend even more money on expensive programs of evangelization, I think we should start with the moments where the Church touches the most people every week: at baptisms, weddings, and funerals. If we did these as well as we possibly can, I am sure that our witness to Christ through his sacraments would bear fruit. To that end, during my opening remarks on these ritual occasions, I always say, "Long gone are the days, thank God, when anyone who is not a Catholic should feel anything but very welcome in this Church today. Whether you are of another Christian denomination, another faith tradition (a Jew, Muslim, Buddhist, or Hindu), or even if you don't share our belief in God, you are very welcome here today, and I hope you will join in all parts of the ceremony you feel you can." This costs me nothing, extends the sort of inclusive hospitality for which the Lord was known, and does untold good. It is certainly far better than starting the liturgy by telling everyone who can and cannot receive Holy Communion. There may be a time to say that very sensitively later in the liturgy, but to start out with who is excluded at the Lord's Table is a pastoral disaster.

Fourth, as I've said in an earlier chapter, our prayer and mission should be all about gratitude. On nearly every world lifestyle indicator, even if we have it rough at present, we live in the most privileged of circumstances. As Christians, we do not think this is our right, our due, or our good fortune. As Christians, we know this is a blessing, and we respond to it every day by just being grateful.

Fifth, our mission must be one of preaching and practicing forgiveness. The two biggest sins that Jesus confronts on nearly every page of the Gospels are hypocrisy, those who say one thing and do another, and refusing to forgive. This part of Jesus' preaching is what set him apart from nearly every other religious leader in history. Jesus kept forgiving people, and he told his disciples to do the same. In following Christ and being on mission, we are never promised an easy ride. In our complex world, no one can pretend that forgiveness is easy, or that it is a magic wand we wave over deep hurts and harsh words. True forgiveness does not deny reality; it deals with it with justice and compassion. But forgiveness is necessary if we are going to follow Jesus. Revenge and spite, so endemic in society, are the antithesis of what Jesus taught and lived out.

Some of us recall the 1970 hit film *Love Story* and its outrageous motto: "Love means never having to say you're sorry." Well, this might have been fine for Ali and Ryan, but let's be very clear: such an attitude is irreconcilable with the Gospel of Jesus Christ. As Christians, exactly the opposite is the case—we look for opportunities to say "I'm sorry" to those we have hurt, and we work toward being the sort of woman or man who can say "I forgive you," without sounding pompous, or being sanctimonious about it. I keep meeting people who have not spoken to family members or friends for years. Clearly, it would be best if they could be reconciled with those who have offended them or those they have hurt, but life is complex. The litmus test for a Christian is whether we even want to, or whether we care. Forgiveness is as much a movement in our heart—we long for reconciliation if it could ever happen—as something that we see realized in this life. So if we are on mission with Christ, then we'd better be like him and become famous for our ability to forgive.

Finally, we will be judged about whether our life in the world is Christian by how we live the three great virtues of faith, hope, and love.

If Christians are those who can naturally say "thank you," "I'm sorry," and "I forgive you," then telling those we love that we love them should also be a normal and natural part of our lives.

But, at least in some cultures and families it's not. Here's a story demonstrating how hard it can be!

When I was seventeen, I read John Powell's *Why Am I Afraid to Love?* At the end of the book, it says that we should never leave this world not having told the people that we love that we love them because if you show how much you love them by what we do and say, then saying it for a Christian should not be difficult. Now, I don't come from a particularly demonstrative family. So I took this challenge personally and seriously.

My sister was then working with Mother Teresa in Calcutta, and my brother was working in another town. I sat down and wrote them letters telling them that I loved them. I never heard back from either of them!

That left my mother. I stayed in one Saturday night, and after dinner, while she was watching the news at seven p.m., I was in my bedroom. I was very nervous. My heart was pumping furiously and my tummy churning badly. You would swear I was about to ask my mother to marry me. I approached the living room and blurted out, "Mum, I have something important to tell you." My mother, not taking her eyes from the screen, casually said, "Oh yes, what's that?" "Mum," I responded, "I've never told you this before, and it's very important that I tell you tonight."

My mother slowly turned off the television and turned toward me. Now I could tell there were two hearts pumping and two tummies churning in that room. Twenty years later my mother told me that at that moment she was saying to herself, "Whatever is coming next, keep calm, keep calm, keep calm."

I plucked up all my courage and came straight out with it. "Mum, I just want to tell you that I love you."

"Is that it?" she asked.

"Yes, before I died I wanted to be able to say that I had told you that I love you," I said.

"Oh God, you're not terminally ill are you?"

"No, no, I hope to die an old man, but before then I wanted to share with you that I actually do love you."

Such was my mother's relief she said, "Goodness me, I hope so," and promptly turned on the television.

I walked all the way back down to my room thinking, I don't think it was meant to go like that. There were no swooning violins, we did not fall into each other's arms, and no statements were made like, "at least one of you three ingrates has turned up at long last to tell me that I'm lovable." None of those things happened at all. What did happen was that my brother and my sister wrote to my mother saying, "We have these very weird letters from Richard. What's the matter with him?" And they all concluded it was phase I was going through. Hopefully, it is a phase I will never get over, because the ease of saying it is at the core of being a Christian.

One of the problems is that we have devalued the currency of the word. We say we love our car, our house, and ice cream. We even say we love our dog or our cat. But we can't love things because they can't love us back. We can only enjoy them. And while we can have deep affection for our pets, they cannot love us as human beings can.

Added to this is how we regularly tell people that we don't love that we love them. That seems to seal the deal. We say "I love you" out of obligation or a bad habit, but we don't actually mean it and we know it. And this doesn't help us when we hear others tell us that we're loved. We may not trust it. I think we should agree only to tell the people that we actually love that we love them. And how do we work out who they are? Jesus' criterion is a very good place to start: for whom would you die? If you just thought about your dog and cat, then you might need therapy immediately. Jesus would have put his life on the line if there were just you and me, so that we might find our way out of the cycle of destruction and death in which we had become entrapped, that we might be saved.

Why bother praying? Because at its best Christian prayer is so utterly practical. It is not about heaven alone, it is about heaven on earth as well. It is not just about saving my soul, but being on mission to the world. And if we have stopped bothering to pray then maybe it is time to start again, or go deeper still, so that we can be the most compassionate, hopeful, joyful, grateful, forgiving, and loving person possible.

If we all lived this out, then our mission to pray and our lives that followed *would* change the world in Christ's name.

Conclusion

In this book I have suggested that one of the reasons some of us give up on prayer is because we may not have been introduced to its riches. Prayer is making space for God to love us, for us to hear that, and then, through the community of faith, to have the courage to return the compliment. It changes lives. The best of prayer engages our vivid imaginations with a vast array of biblical images to develop a set of ideas that reflect various personal theologies for God that will suit every season under the sun. One size does not fit all. This enables us to enter more deeply into a relationship with God who accompanies us through the events of our lives.

We pray because prayer is not just about asking for something for someone, somewhere. Intercessory prayer is important given that it asks an unchanging God to change us to change the world, but also because it helps to see that the psalms are in fact a workshop showing us how to explore other deeply human responses to the divine: praising and giving thanks; crying out in lamentation; affirming our trust and faith; singing of our salvation; and simply waiting upon the Lord.

Building on the scriptures, our Christian heritage has given us a supermarket of ideas, styles, insights, challenges, and ways and means to God. For many people, the schools of prayer provide a history, framework, discipline, meaning, and structure to their communication with God and one another. The schools connect them to something that has stood the test of time and helped millions of people, not just to have deeper prayer lives, but also to transform their community for the better by how they have lived.

No matter what image, response, or school of prayer we find helpful, Christian prayer is centered on a person, Jesus, and through him, we are invited into a loving and saving relationship with the Father, Son, and Spirit that has consequences for how we live in this world and the next. In this relationship, nothing is wasted in our often-complex lives. We are invited to grow from where we are, as we are, to realize our full potential. Prayer helps us face down fear, and live in hope. And when we feel distant from Jesus, guess who has moved away from whom? Our prayer is not about appeasing an angry God. There is nothing that can ever, or will ever, stop God from loving us.

Because Christian faith is personal but never private, then public prayer matters because I am not just saved as an individual, but we are saved as the people of God. We need each other to rise to that invitation as we come together to pray in an assembly that stands before mystery, in awe and wonder, is hospitable, and expresses ancient faith in a contemporary world. In the sacraments, God's greatness meets our frailty. Mary and the saints show us how it's done and always lead us to Christ. And most of us need all the help we can get. We need role models who have said "yes" as they made their own pilgrimage of faith and hung in there when the going got tough, especially when they touched their own personal, spiritual, and sometimes material poverty.

Prayer comes at a price. It is not a spiritual *bon mot*. We do not pray simply to effect our salvation in heaven. We pray to keep on mission with Christ in the world. Our lives may be the only Bible some people will ever read. Our living of the virtues and our commitment to justice and peace may be the only sacraments some people will ever witness and celebrate. They might decide whether to bother praying based on what they hear but even more, what they see. Our prayer is not to be judged on how we feel, but on how we live and what we say away from prayer. We do not need to babble. Let's put an end to performances for God. We do not need to have our head in the clouds. Prayer is practical. Though we all fail, prayerful people are traced with Christ's life because of the encounter with him and so are compassionate, hopeful, joyful, grateful, forgiving, and loving. The Church and the world need prayerful people more than ever before.

Even though some people say we are mad, that we are talking to our imaginary friends, those of us who have experienced God's love in prayer and have made the decision to believe within the community of the Church know the adventure of faith is worth the risk, and even the hostility, because of the sense of purpose and meaning prayer gives us.

Why bother praying? Because God wants us to bother him, and in the process develop a relationship that is marked by such love and joy that it changes us, our neighbor, and the world.

Bibliography

Abbott, Walter M. (ed.). *The Documents of Vatican II*, America Press, 2012.

Barry, William A. *A Friendship Like No Other: Experiencing God's Amazing Embrace*, Loyola Press, 2008.

————. *God and You: Prayer as a Personal Relationship*, Paulist Press, 1987.

————. *Praying the Truth: Deepening Your Friendship with God through Honest Prayer*. Loyola Press, 2002.

Bell, John L. *Cloth for the Cradle*, Iona Community, GIA, 1997, 2001.

Borg, Marcus. *The God We Never Knew: Beyond Dogmatic Religion to a More Authentic Contemporary Faith*, Harper One, 1998.

Chittister, Joan. *The Rule of Benedict: Insights for the Ages*, Crossroads, 1992.

Congregation for the Doctrine of the Faith. *The Norms Regarding the Manner of Proceeding in the Discernment of Presumed Apparitions or Revelations*, Vatican City, 1978.

Dupré, Louis. *The Other Dimension*, Doubleday, 1972.

Fitzmyer, Joseph A. *The Gospel According to Luke*, Doubleday, 1982.

Leonard, Richard. *Beloved Daughters: 100 Years of Papal Teaching about Women*, Novalis, 1996.

————. *Movies That Matter: Reading Film Through Faith*, Loyola Press, 2006.

————. *Preaching to the Converted*, Paulist Press, 2007.

————. *The Mystical Gaze: The Films of Peter Weir*, Melbourne University Press, 2009.

————. *Where the Hell Is God?* Paulist Press, 2010.

Madigan, Daniel A. "When Experience Leads to Different Beliefs," *The Way Supplement* 92, 1998, pp. 65–74.

Maréchal, Joseph. *Studies in the Psychology of the Mystics*, Magi Books, 1964.

Maritain, Jacques. *The Degrees of Knowledge*, Charles Scribner, 1959.

Martin, James. *Between Heaven and Mirth*, Harper One, 2011.

————. *The Jesuit Guide to Almost Everything*, Harper One, 2012.

McKay, Ryan. "Hallucinating God? The Cognitive Neuropsychiatry of Religious Belief and Experience," *Evolution and Cognition* 10 (1), 114–125, 2004.

Paul VI. *Marialis Cultus: For the Right Ordering and Development of Devotion to the Blessed Virgin Mary*, Vatican City, February 2, 1974.

Santayana, George. *The Life of Reason or The Phases of Human Progress: Introduction and Reason in Common Sense*, Volume VII, Book One (The Works of George Santayana) (Volume 7), The MIT Press, 2001.

Sorkin, Aaron. "Two Cathedrals" (Episode 44), *The West Wing: The Complete Series Collection* (2006), Warner Home Video, 2006.

The Catechism of the Catholic Church, Image, 1995.

Wallace, Frank. *Encounter, Not Performance*, EJ Dwyer, 1991.

WEB SITES

www.IgnatianSpirituality.com
www.pray-as-you-go.org
www.sacredspace.com
www.smilegodlovesyou.org/names.htm

Films upon Which to Pray

Agnes of God (1985). Directed by Norman Jewison. Mature audiences, supernatural and adult themes. 90 minutes.

In a cloistered convent near Montreal, a young novice gives birth to a child in her room and it dies. The superior finds the baby wrapped in a towel in the wastebasket. The authorities suspect that Sister Agnes of God has murdered the infant. Various options are explored about how she came to be pregnant, but the court cannot rule out that she is mystic and has been touched by God. A sophisticated exploration of mysticism, hysteria, and prayer.

As It Is in Heaven (*Så som i himmelen*) (2004). Directed by Kay Pollak. Moderate coarse language, moderate themes, a sex scene, moderate violence. 127 minutes.

A drama about exorcising demons and discovering love. Daniel Darius, an internationally recognized conductor, drops out of international celebrity after a heart attack and steps back into his childhood village in the far north of Sweden. A film all about obedience—attuning the ear to listen—from which comes harmony and balance. Keep your eye out for the angels in this film. They are everywhere.

Babette's Feast (1987). Directed by Gabriel Axel. General audience. 102 minutes.

Babette escapes the Parisian riots to a remote village in Denmark, where she becomes the cook for two sisters. She ends up cooking a thanksgiving feast for the village. This film can be read as parable of Eucharistic hospitality and as a homage to an artist, in this case a culinary artist. Keep your eye out for how

Babette's full story is only gradually revealed: the sisters are like Mary and Martha of Bethany, Babette gives everything for her friends, and the meal has the power to transform lives, to tell the truth, to forgive, and to prefigure the eternal banquet.

Billy Elliott (2000). Directed by Stephen Daldry. Mature themes, frequent coarse language, and some violence. 110 minutes.

In the North of England, Billy is sent off to the local hall to learn boxing. He hates it, so he joins the ballet class next door and finds his real talent. When his father finds out, his ideas about masculinity are shaken up. He has to decide to support Billy and how to raise money for his audition in London. This film is a study in the anatomy of discernment, the demands of love, and a God of surprises.

Bruce Almighty (1993). Directed by Tom Shadyac. Low-level coarse language and low-level violence. 94 minutes.

Bruce blames God for his misfortune and so God challenges him to do a better job. This is a great allegory about original sin, where we rebel at being a creature and want to be the Creator. This is a very engaging, if occasionally crude look at the nature of prayer, what grace is and does, and the power of the poor to tell us the truth.

It cannot resolve many of the complex questions it proposes, so it turns to an appallingly schmaltzy ending to finish off the film, but it is a brave attempt to ask the most basic religious questions in a modern context. "The problem is that people keep looking up, when they should look inside….You want to see a miracle—then be a miracle."

Chariots of Fire (1981). Directed by Hugh Hudson. Infrequent violence. 123 minutes.

The story of the 100-yard dash at the 1924 Olympics at Paris, focuses on Eric Liddell, a Scotsman who is a missionary in his evangelical Christian church, and on Harold Abrahams, the son of a Jewish migrant. This film is about finding God in all things, including our bodies, and athletic prowess as a gift from God to be used as tool for evangelization. "I believe God made me for a purpose, but he also made me fast. And when I run I feel His pleasure....Where does the power come from, to see the race to its end? From within."A fascinating, if flawed study on obeying one's conscience.

The Chronicles of Narnia: The Lion, the Witch and the Wardrobe (2005), Prince Caspian (2008), The Voyage of the Dawn Treader (2011), The Silver Chair (2012). Various directors. Mild fantasy violence, some frightening scenes, battle violence. Various running times.

It is entirely possible, of course, to enjoy these wonderful movies as vivid fantasies or as allegories about the defeat of Nazi evil in World War II or even about the medieval Christian crusades to reclaim the Holy Land (Narnia). However, the four films so far with three more slated to come (*The Horse and His Boy*; *The Magician's Nephew*; *The Last Battle*) can easily be read as an extended Christian parable. Writer C. S. Lewis said that we could imagine "parallel worlds, and that in one of them the Son of God, as He became Man in our world, became a Lion there, and then imagine what would happen." Great themes here about "things never happen the same way twice," trust, learning from experiences, holding to faith in the face of insurmountable odds, believing in hope, and the centrality of the imagination.

Dead Man Walking (1995). Directed by Tim Robbins. Adult themes and medium-level violence. 122 minutes.

Based on an autobiography of Sr. Helen Prejean, *Dead Man Walking* is the story of a nun who accompanies a man to his death by lethal injection. It is a study in pastoral care, and human empathy, in never allowing anyone to be seen as a monster, in holding to a faith that no one is beyond God's redemption, and in our ability to forgive. Revenge can look so satisfying but rarely leads to peace. Forgiveness does not deny things were done, but rises to say that despite what was done, I still forgive you. Sometimes we ask the question, "What would Jesus do?" This film gives us the answer.

Dead Poets Society (1989). Directed by Peter Weir. Mature themes and occasional violence. 128 minutes.

A film that places two wonderful phrases on modern lips has a lot going for it: *"Carpe diem"* ("Seize the day") and "Suck the marrow out of life." As the film tragically shows, there can be terrible consequences when we live out other people's dreams, or we try to make others live out ours. This film helps us to ask what we really want in life, who we want to be, and to go after it. This is not far from Jesus asking, "Who are you looking for? Come and see," and later, "I have come that you might have life and have to the full."

Departures. (2008) Directed by Yojiro Takita. Mature themes. 101 minutes.

The winner of the 2008 Oscar for Best Foreign Film, the film opens with the ritual for the dead. Daigo, who is an unemployed cello player, becomes a "coffinator," an embalmer of the dead. This film confronts our fear of death and separation with grace and style and humor. It is a very healing and comforting film for anyone in grief.

The Diving Bell and the Butterfly (2007). Directed by Julian Schnabel. Adult themes and nudity. 112 minutes.

Jean-Dominique Bauby awakens to find he is in a hospital, hooked up to machines to help him breathe. He has had a cerebral-vascular accident and has "locked-in syndrome"—only his left eyelid is functional. He wants to die but cannot kill himself. He wants to find hope but there is only depression, and then an angel of light assists him to find meaning in suffering. This powerful film is based on a true story.

The End of the Affair (1999). Directed by Neil Jordan. Adult themes, nudity, and sex scenes. 102 minutes.

Graham Greene was one of the most celebrated converts to Catholicism in the 1950s. This film is an adaptation of his thinly veiled autobiographical work of the same name, concerning a love affair between Maurice Bendrix and Sarah Miles toward the end of World War II, in spite of the fact that Sarah is married to Henry Miles. Like many of Greene's novels, this film deals with personal morality, ethical choices, the consequences of deceit and compromise, and that the wages of sin are death.

Entertaining Angels: The Dorothy Day Story (1996). Directed by Michael Ray Rhodes. Mature themes. 110 minutes.

Dorothy Day was the joint founder with Peter Maurin of The Catholic Worker. She is considered by many today to be a saint, but as yet uncanonized. This biopic shows how hard-won her conversion to Catholicism actually was, and why she believed in the power of forgiveness and compassion for the rest her life.

Harry Potter Series (2001, 2002, 2004, 2005, 2007, 2009, 2011). Various directors. Supernatural themes, medium level horror violence, fantasy scenes. Various running times.

Harry is a boy wizard who has to learn his craft and discover his destiny. These films have been criticized for introducing children to the world of occult, for sugarcoating Satanism, and for domesticating evil. If we take that commentary seriously, we would never again read fables, fairy stories, or Macbeth because it has witches. Does anyone know anyone who became a Satanist as result of Harry Potter? In fact, these films portray the way in which we have to learn discernment between good and evil. They are mystical parables with allegories about the Prophet Daniel, the cost of standing up and being counted for doing the moral thing, the reality of evil, and ultimately that good will have the last word.

Hotel Rwanda (2005). Directed by Terry George. Adult themes, medium level violence, low-level coarse language. 121 minutes.

Rather than focus on the horrors of the Rwandan genocide, this film tells the true story of Paul Rusesabagina, the manager of a Belgian-owned hotel in Kigali, who although he is a Hutu, saved over a thousand Tutsi lives. Paul is a compassionate and intelligent man who is forced by circumstances to make a series of moral choices that sets him ineluctably on the path to becoming a hero. It is also one of the best portrayals of fidelity and self-sacrifice in Christian marriage you are likely to see. Be warned, however, it is not set amidst genocide without consequences.

The Hurricane (1999). Directed by Norman Jewison. Coarse language, low-level violence, adult themes. 146 minutes.

This is the true story of Rubin "Hurricane" Carter, the greatest boxer that never was. He was falsely accused of murder and left to rot in jail for twenty-two years. That is until Lesra, a young, struggling, African-American man reads a book about Rubin and begins corresponding with him. Lesra encourages his friends Terry, Lisa, and Sam to join him in a fresh campaign for Carter's release. A film that shows how evil racism is; what constitutes freedom and who is entrapped; following one's conscience; the cause for justice; the importance of friendship; and the power of words—written, read, and spoken. Keep your ear out for the biblical names throughout. They are all true, but could not have been better chosen than if by a fictional author.

Jesus of Montreal (1989). Directed by Denys Arcand. Occasional coarse language. 119 minutes. Adult concepts.

This film is a study in "quotation," where the play within a play, after a fashion, tells a version of Jesus' life. Keep your eye out for John the Baptist, the calling of the poor as disciples, the cleansing of the temple, the debate between science and reason, the quest for the historical Jesus, how Jesus has nowhere to lay his head, the Mary Magdalene figure, the mysterious Daniel, the woman caught in the "very act" of adultery, the mountain top, the Palm Sunday crowd, predictions of the Passion, the temptations in the desert, the Last Supper, the arrest in the garden, how the men flee but the women remain faithful, dissent among the dead, Judas in the subway, the Sacred Heart, the imperfect metaphor of resurrection in transplantation. It is a film that likes Jesus but rails against the institutional Church.

Jesus of Nazareth (1978). Directed by Franco Zefferelli. Mild themes and violence. 372 minutes.

This is the finest of the classical Jesus films. Made as a TV miniseries, it is also very long. The good news is that this film can be successfully shown in blocks or even scenes, and some of them are masterpieces: the annunciation; the scourging at the pillar where we don't see Jesus being whipped but hear it as we watch horses in the stables who know what it is to be scourged rear up in their stalls; and the crucifixion, especially the taking down of the body.

The Last Days (1998). Documentary film directed by James Moll. Adult themes. 88 minutes.

One of the most moving documentaries I have ever seen. It is not just about five Hungarian Jews who were children when they were deported to the death camps. It is like a biblical narrative: the story of scapegoat theology, purification of memory, handing on the story: "They are not going to take my soul....I am not going to ashes," "Where is God? God is in your strength," "God did not create the Holocaust...God gave us free will. I blame men not God."

The Lives of Others (2006). Directed by Florian Henckel von Donnersmarck. Adult themes, strong sexual references, a sex scene. 137 mins.

The Lives of Others won the Oscar for the Best Foreign Film in 2007. Set in East Germany of 1984, five years before the

Berlin Wall collapsed. Stasi Captain Gerd Wiesler eavesdrops on Maria Sieland, a popular and very attractive actress, as well as on the country's most loyal playwright, Georg Dreyman. In the process of spying for the state, he falls out of love with his country and in love with truth, dignity, and justice. Not even a lifetime of indoctrination and the intimate knowledge of the consequences of his betrayal if he's caught by the State obliterates the spark of goodness in him. None of us is beyond God's grace.

The Lord of the Rings Series. *The Fellowship of the Ring* (2001); *The Two Towers* (2002); *The Return of the King* (2003). Directed by Peter Jackson. Supernatural themes and medium-level violence. Various running times.

J.R.R. Tolkien wrote these works as a statement of Christian faith in the face of the horror of war. "…The Lord of the Rings is of course a fundamentally religious and Catholic work; unconsciously so at first but consciously in the revision…." *The Lord of the Rings* can easily be seen as an allegory on the eventual reign of Christ the King at the Parousia. There are also three Christ figures: Gandalf (who dies and rises again); Frodo who is the ringbearer, traveling along the Via Dolorosa, like Christ with the cross; and Strider/Aragon who is the hidden king, finally revealed in triumph. Keep a good eye on the most creative portrayal of the Trinity on the big screen: Gandalf is the Father who creates and calls; Frodo is the Son who takes on the form of the least, a hobbit, but whose destiny is to save; and Galadriel is the Spirit who inspires, enlightens, and comforts. There are also very rich lessons about how fatigue and desire can see us make poor choices, and that if we give into our worst choices we can become them, like Gollum.

Lourdes (2009). Directed by Jessica Hausner. General audience. 96 minutes

Christine has severe multiple sclerosis and is paralyzed. She makes a pilgrimage with a group to Lourdes in the hope of a cure. This stunning film is not just about a journey to Lourdes in France, but the journey of faith, dealing with miracles, the nature of prayer, and the question of if there is a God of love whether he is "fair" by healing some but not others.

Millions (2004). Directed by Danny Boyle. Mature themes, mild coarse language, and mild sexual references. 98 minutes.

Damien's best friends are in the Communion of Saints. He knows them intimately and they love him. He wants to know if his mother is in heaven with them. This contemporary British film shows better than any I have seen the way we can befriend saints as our companions and role models. It has good lessons about greed and avarice and how we become the choices we make.

The Mission (1986). Directed by Roland Joffe. Adult themes, some violence. 125 minutes.

The conflated story of the Paraguayan Reductions in 1750. Great themes here of how the wages of sin are death, and of repentance, conversion, penance, forgiveness. Fr. Gabriel says, "If might is right, then love has no place in the world. It may be so, it may be so. But I don't have the strength to live in a world like that, Rodrigo." In *The Mission* he raises several questions worthy of prayerful reflection: Do we really believe in personal and social conversion? Was missionary activity always destructive for local cultures? Are pride, riches, and greed the motivation for our most destructive behavior? When is it justifiable to take up arms and fight?

Molokai: The Story of Father Damien (1999). Directed by Irwin Winkler. Adult themes. 120 minutes.

Father (now Saint) Damien was celebrated for his fidelity to the lepers on the Hawaiian Island of Molokai. Even though there are problems with this uneven film, it portrays the nature of sacrificial love, not just that of Fr. Damien, but also of Mother (now Saint) Maryanne Cope and her sisters. It is the story of the wounded healers. It also asks us to think about how we still hide the poor away from view.

Monsieur Lazhar (2012). Directed by Phillippe Falardeau. Mature themes. 95 minutes.

This film is based on the one-character play by Evelyne de la Cheneliere, *Bachir Lazhar*; the name *Bachir* means "the bearer of good news." After the suicide of a teacher in a Montreal school, an Algerian refugee immigrant, Bachir Lazhar, is sent in as the substitute teacher. He has suffered greatly and is just the person to offer the children hope in their despair, healing for their pain, and proof that there can be life after death.

Monty Python's Life of Brian (1979). Directed by Eric Idle. Strong coarse language; satirical humor. 90 minutes.

Another film that likes Jesus but is implicitly critical of the Church. The film never explicitly parodies Jesus. He is a character in the film, but is always treated with respect. It is the interpretation around Jesus, religious intolerance, the expectations about the Messiah and his message, and the process by which signs are interpreted that come in for lampooning. It is not an anti-Christ film. It is an anti-Church film. It is the best film I know about religious hermeneutics, the process of interpretation.

Nader and Simin, a Separation (2012). Directed by Asghar Farhadi. Mild themes and coarse language. 118 minutes.

This Iranian film, which won the Ecumenical Jury Prize at the Berlin International Film Festival, is about an Iranian middle-class couple going through the process of being divorced. Simin wants to leave Iran. Nader wants to stay and care for his elderly father. He hires Razieh, who is pregnant, as caregiver. After an argument with Razieh, Nader pushes her, and she falls and suffers a miscarriage. He is accused of murder. Everything is here: parent-child relations, separation, moral decision-making, justice, and religious commitment.

The Name of the Rose (1998). Directed by Jen-Jacques Annaud. Adult themes, mild violence, sex scene. 124 minutes.

In the fourteenth century the monks of a Benedictine monastery in the north of Italy are dying. The abbot calls for the famous Franciscan theologian William of Baskerville to investigate. He brings his young novice Adso of Melk. Later, the Dominican inquisitor, Bernardo Gui, arrives. Underlining the film and the book is the interplay between sex and death, two of the powerful, irresistible forces that human beings have to deal with. We can try to ignore them, repress them, and cheat them, but they will have the last word. The more they are seen as integral to human nature, are dealt with in the open, and are each seen as gifts, in vastly differing ways, the more constructive their role can be in our human personalities and spiritual lives as well. The film argues that humor is one of the best ways to approach sex and death. Neither are frivolous matters, but humor keeps us grounded in reality about our humanity in the first case, and Christ's divinity in the second.

Of Gods and Men (2011). Written and directed by Xavier Beauvois. A strong violent scene. 183 minutes.

One of the finest religious and best Catholic films of all time. This slow-paced but moving film portrays the life and ministry of the Trappist community of Mt. Atlas, Algeria, in the 1990s. When Islamic extremists invade the area, the monks have to discern whether they should stay with their people or return to their native France.

Romero (1989). Directed by John Duigan. Some violence. 102 minutes.

A biopic about the Archbishop of San Salvador who was assassinated in 1977. He was the most unlikely of social prophets, but became the voice of the poor against the military junta. "I want to make a special appeal to soldiers, national guardsmen, and policemen: each of you is one of us. The peasants you kill are your own brothers and sisters. When you hear a man telling you to kill, remember God's words, 'Thou shalt not kill.' No soldier is obliged to obey a law contrary to the law of God. In the name of God, in the name of our tormented people, I beseech you, I implore you; in the name of God I command you to stop the repression." A moving film about martyrdom and the cost of following Jesus.

The Shawshank Redemption (1994). Directed by Frank Darabont. High-level coarse language and medium level violence. 142 minutes.

Andy Dufresne, falsely jailed for his wife's murder, plots his escape from an evil jail. "Andy Dufresne—who crawled through a river of shit and came out clean on the other side." Andy tells Red Redding, his fellow inmate and best friend, to meet him on the beach at Zihuatenejo in Mexico when he gets out. Andy is a Christ figure, an innocent man who is wrongly convicted and persecuted, but who nonetheless sets others free by how he lives his life. Against the odds, and even when the truth lets him down, Andy believes in hope and beauty. The final scene is a parallel of John 21:4–8, where the Risen Christ meets the disciples on the beach. Zihuatenejo is heaven by another name.

The Truman Show (1998). Directed by Peter Weir. Adult themes and low-level coarse language. 103 minutes.

When this film came out in 1998 parodying real-life television, people thought it was a fantasy. Given everything we have seen since then, this film looks prophetic. However, *The Truman Show* does not just provide searing social commentary. This film provides the model of how many people imagine God sitting in the control room in the sky calling the shots on earth. At heart, *The Truman Show* is liberation, and it can be freedom from a false image of God, from an unrealistic world, and about being free to embrace our life and live it.

Turtles Can Fly (2004). Written and directed by Bahman Ghobadi. Adult themes and low-level violence. 98 minutes.

In a refugee camp on the Turkish/Iranian border, a growing community of Kurdish refugees is caught between Saddam Hussein's genocide on one side, and Iran's refusal to let them cross into their territory on the other. In this community a near-sighted thirteen-year-old orphaned boy is the king of the castle. This confronting film enables us to pray about a world where our lives are, in global terms, so blest while others, through no fault of their own, have so little. With humor and humanity it provides a gentle window into a world we know so little about, and yet one to which we are intimately linked, whether we like it or not. In surprising ways, this film challenges our thinking in regard to our countries' attitudes and policies toward war, refugees, and who receives our compassion.

The Visitor (2008). Directed by Thomas McCarthy. Infrequent coarse language. 109 minutes.

A sixtyish widower who lectures at a Connecticut college has withdrawn into himself and into the stale routines of academia. His main attempt to come out of himself, to learn to play the piano, comes to nothing. When he finds two illegal immigrants occupying his New York apartment, he is shocked but offers them some temporary refuge. When one of them, Tarek, is suddenly detained, it has a profound effect on Walter who makes many efforts on his behalf. This film is all about conversion on a personal and social level. Conversion changes the way we see everything.

The Way (2011). Directed by Emilio Estevez. Mild themes, drug use, and coarse language. 123 minutes.

A fictional story about eccentric, deeply wounded characters who make The Camino, the pilgrimage to Santiago de

Compestella in northern Spain, together and along the way deal with the anger, grief, hurt, and pain that unconsciously caused them to begin it in the first place. The insightful tag line of the film comes from Daniel's challenge to his father as he takes flight from home: "You don't choose a life, Dad. You live one." An even more telling line comes later: "The Camino is all about confronting death."

Whale Rider (2002). Directed by Niki Caro. Adult themes and low-level coarse language. 103 minutes.

The Whangara people in New Zealand say their leader Paikea came from Hawaii riding on the back of a whale. Ever since, the first-born male descendants of the Paikea clan have been the chiefs of the tribe. Set in contemporary New Zealand, the present claimant to leadership is a girl, Paikea. A simple and profound film about traditions, patriarchy, the power of women, and the pain of transition. This story highlights that while men may be the only ones allowed to be ordained, that does not stop Christ from raising up his sisters to be some of our greatest leaders.

Witness (1985). Directed by Peter Weir. Mature audiences. 110 minutes.

Only Peter Weir could frame a thriller and a romance in an Amish community. On the way, he explores critical spiritual themes about community, truth-telling, ritual, and the mysticism of hard work and living close to the earth. A gentle refutation of Western secular values, *Witness* asks us what we witness to, and to whom we are witnessing. This film is an exploration of what it means to be faithful.